40 day
sales
DARE

for
New Home Sales

JASON FORREST

author of *Creating Urgency in a Non-Urgent Housing Market*

For information or bulk orders, contact:
info@ShoreForrest.com

www.40DaySalesDare.com

Printed by Branch-Smith Printing
Fort Worth, Texas

International Standard Book Number: 0-9801762-2-0 (10 digit)
                                    978-0-9801762-2-3 (13 digit)

Acknowledgements

To Alicia Sample, the editor who took my ideas to a higher level.

To Kara Libick, the designer who created a visually appealing layout through her sense of style.

To Jeff Shore, my business partner who holds me accountable to being the best version of me at work and in life.

To my kids, Saunders and Mary Jane, who remind me every day to have a childlike curiosity by always asking, "Why?"

To Shelly, my wife, who cheered me on while writing this book. Through your love and support, anything is possible.

To all the people out there who have chosen to read this book: you are the real professionals out there investing in yourselves, not in circumstance!

Contents

* *Indicates that this Dare is a Day-Off Dare, meant to be executed when you are out of the office. See the chapter "How to Use This Book" for details.*

This isn't a typical book intro - be sure to read it.

Dear Salesperson,

Are you ready to reach your full potential, regardless of which community you've been given, what market you're in, or how many urgent buyers walk through your door each week? My vision for *40 Day Sales Dare* is to help you increase your income by giving you specific tasks and goals for the next forty days. If you aren't interested in increasing your current earnings, then this book might not be right for you. But, if you are like most goal-oriented, performance-driven salespeople, you want to earn more. The book you're holding will help you do just that by challenging you to achieve the best version of yourself every day. Whether there was something deep inside of you that said, "I need that book," or you received it as a gift and/or assignment, this book found you to help you earn what you're worth!

Since your current performance is returning your current results, you can either keep doing everything the same way, and wait for circumstances to tilt more in your favor, or you can change your behaviors and therefore change your results. This book will help you change your behaviors, but you have a part in it, too.

In order to get the most from this book, I want you to focus on the following:

Take it one day at a time.

Rather than focusing on reaching the end of this book, the end of the quarter, or the end of the year, just commit to reading each day's Dare before you start your day, and to executing it to the best of your ability. This means that, after you read the day's chapter, you spend time on the *Think* section, then execute the Dare mentally and physically throughout the day. Finally, in the *Reflect* section, you will reflect on the results of the Dare and ask yourself how you can improve.

See your only competitor as yourself.

Focus only on you and on your own game. Don't worry about your performance in comparison to anyone else's.

When you compare yourself to others, you get in trouble because you either think they are better than you, or you think you are better than they are. It's dangerous to worry about who is better, because you're defeated before you even begin, thinking that you will never become that good. You lose hope in your own potential and give yourself an unhealthy excuse not to challenge yourself. It's just as unhealthy to think you are better than someone else because you set a ceiling of what's possible for you, and think things like, "I'm selling 20% more than everyone else on my team—that must be good enough." Why would that be good enough if you could do better?

Make it your goal to push yourself to be better—to be your best. Your success is linear—as you improve your sales behaviors and beliefs, you improve your earnings, too.

Focus on each customer as if he/she is your only customer.

Give each customer the best version of you. Make a commitment to each prospect, before they come in, that you are going to give them the best experience you can, and then live it out. Slow down with every customer you meet and focus on taking that prospect as far in the sales process as you can. But don't stop there—when they leave, study what you did well and what you could do better with your next client.

Eliminate all excuses.

I don't care if you see thirty customers a day or zero, you must practice each Dare each day. If you have thirty customers, perfect! Practice three times before anyone shows up, and then execute the Dare with each one of your prospects. You'll be a pro by the end. If you have zero customers, perfect! Practice the Dare mentally, with your sales partner, and with the bobble head on your desk. Visualize each specific technique in great detail—what you would say, what the customer would say in return, and what the results would be. By the time a customer experiences the Dare with you, you'll already be comfortable with it.

While we're at it, eliminate any excuse that pops into your head about why you can't perform fully or why you can't practice each Dare. Instead of finding excuses, find *solutions*. Make a commitment for the next forty days of your life not to worry about what can't be done, and not to say (or even think) that it's impossible to sell more in your situation.

One last thought.

As I said in my first book, *Creating Urgency in a Non-Urgent Housing Market*, the desire to improve one's life has more influence over a person's buying decision than any other factor. Just the same, I believe that the desire to improve your life has more influence over your decisions than any other factor. So focus on how your life and your family's life will be better when you are better. Focus not on what you perceive as "impossible" in your circumstances, but rather on how to make things possible.

In the end, give me forty days of your life, and let's see what happens together.

Your Sales Coach,
Jason

Very important – do not skip!

How to Use This Book

Set up

This book is designed to be used for forty successive days. That means that every morning (whether you work or not) you will have a Dare to focus on for that day.

Let's start with some vocabulary. For the purposes of this book, **Days On** are scheduled work days spent inside the sales office, and **Days Off** are those days when you are not scheduled to work. **Day-On Dares** are designed to be executed and practiced right there in the real-world office situation, while most **Day-Off Dares** can be done from anywhere.

Let's Get Technical

The book is divided into six weeks. At the beginning of each week, you will see a page that lists the week's Dares: *five Day-On Dares*, and *two Day-Off Dares*. This page is important because it helps you to plan your week and determine which Dare you should focus on each day. Here is an example of what that page will look like:

Week 1
Dares 1-7

Day-On Dares

_____ 1. A Spoonful of Sugar

_____ 2. All She Wanted was a Little Black Dress

_____ 3. Show Up

_____ 4. Plot a Course

_____ 5. Pick the Right Song

Day-Off Dares

_____ 6. Why Not?

_____ 7. It's Not a Used Tissue

To use this page, you will fill in your work schedule accordingly. I'm going to walk you through this, but first let me give you an example of how this works. Let's assume that Mr. Salesperson starts *40 Day Sales Dare* on a Monday, and his days off are Tuesday and Wednesday. Mr. Salesperson would write his first "on" day next to the first Day-On Dare, which is *Dare 1*. Since his days off are Tuesday and Wednesday, he'll then jump to the Day-Off Dares and write those days down. Mr. Salesperson will then return to work on Thursday and pick back up with *Dare 2*, continuing through to *Dare 5* on Sunday. See below:

Week 1 for Mr. Salesperson
Dares 1-7

Day-On Dares

Mon 1. A Spoonful of Sugar

Thu 2. All She Wanted was a Little Black Dress

Fri 3. Show Up

Sat 4. Plot a Course

Sun 5. Pick the Right Song

Day-Off Dares

he writes his days off here

Tue 6. Why Not?

Wed 7. It's Not a Used Tissue

So to put it simply, each week you have seven Dares to complete—there are five for your days on, and two for your days off. Each week you need to take a few seconds to plan your customized schedule for completing the seven Dares*. Now it's time for you to practice. I'll walk you through Week 1:

Step 1: Choose the day when you will begin *40 Day Sales Dare*. Be sure to choose a day when you will be in the office.

Step 2: Write that day next to the first Day-On Dare of the week.

Step 3: Continue writing your "on" days next to the Day-On Dares, until you come to your days off for the week.

Step 4: Write your "off" days next to the Day-Off Dares.

Step 5: Finish filling in your "on" days for the week.

Week 1 for You
Dares 1-7

Day-On Dares

_____ 1. A Spoonful of Sugar

_____ 2. All She Wanted was a Little Black Dress

_____ 3. Show Up

_____ 4. Plot a Course

_____ 5. Pick the Right Song

Day-Off Dares

_____ 6. Why Not?

_____ 7. It's Not a Used Tissue

You've written your schedule for the first week! Unless your days off change, you will probably stick to this same schedule each week throughout *40 Day Sales Dare*. If you want, you can turn to page 17 to copy your schedule down, and then ***return to page 14 for further instruction***.

---

* *Week 6 will only have five Dares.*

What if I miss a day?

If you miss a day of work, you can adjust your *40 Day* schedule accordingly. Or, you can stay on the schedule you've created, and commit to making up the Dare that you missed after you've completed *Dare 40*. Whatever you decide to do, make sure that you only complete Day-On Dares when you're in the office, and Day-Off Dares when you're not.

T r a c k i n g   Y o u r   P r o g r e s s

When participating in any self-improvement program, it is vital that you track your progress. You need to chart your successes and your shortcomings in order to know where you are, where you need to go, and what you need to do in order to get there.

In *40 Day Sales Dare*, you are going to track two important factors of your self-improvement: Effort and Potential Value.

Effort

Each Dare concludes with an Effort Scale. You will be asked to rate the Effort that you gave to executing the day's Dare—truthfully and realistically. The purpose of this scale is to help you keep tabs on your commitment to the program. When you see yourself slipping, you can take corrective measures right away, and recommit yourself to your self-improvement.

$ Potential Value $

At the end of each Dare, you will also be asked, "What was this week worth to you?" That is, if you were to faithfully execute the Dare, about how many sales do you think it would earn you over the next year? You will circle a value in a scale that looks like this:

14

```
.25 sales    .5 sales    .75 sales    1 sale
1.25 sales   1.5 sales   1.75 sales   2 sales
```

The purpose of this measurement is to help you focus on the future rewards that you will gain as a result of your efforts. Some Dares will be challenging, and will stretch you beyond your comfort zone, but if you can focus on the future rewards of the sales you will earn, you will be inspired to keep pressing forward in your journey toward self-improvement and success.

At the end of each week, you will see a **Summary page** where you will be asked to calculate the average scores for your Effort and your Potential Value. *It is critical that you complete this page.* When you see your averages, you will know what kind of measures you need to take in order to conquer the next week. Doing this summary is kind of like stepping on the scale every week to make sure that your diet and exercise routine is working—it's easier to make adjustments to lose one extra pound than it is to get back on the wagon four weeks later and attempt to lose the six pounds that mysteriously appeared.

Totaling Your Potential

At the end of the book, you will be provided a page where you will calculate the total Potential Value of all forty Dares. You will be able to say, "If I were to implement everything in this book, I would earn ___ sales this year." Seeing this number in print will give you the motivation you need to take the Dares to heart, and to continue practicing them until you've mastered the concepts and strategies they teach.

*   *   *

Now that you know how to use this book, it's time to get started. I hope you are ready for a journey that will change your life.

Week 1

Dares 1-7

Day-On Dares

_____ 1. A Spoonful of Sugar

_____ 2. All She Wanted Was a Little Black Dress

_____ 3. Show Up

_____ 4. Plot a Course

_____ 5. Pick the Right Song

Day-Off Dares

_____ 6. Why Not?

_____ 7. It's Not a Used Tissue!

"Give the customer a chance to become emotionally connected before you say that it's out of their price range."

Dare 1

A Spoonful of Sugar

read

Picture this: a guy approaches a girl to ask her out. He says, "Hi, my name is Steve and I drink too much, smoke at least a pack of cigarettes a day, and eat more than I should. I don't work out and I will forget your birthday and major holidays. I won't be friends with your friends, but I expect you to be friends with mine. Oh, and one more thing. You must cook every meal." How likely is Steve to get a date? Even if these things are true about Steve, he has to get his potential date emotionally interested in him before he gives her reason to hate him.

It sounds extreme, but I see salespeople do this all the time. They bring up all the stressful topics like credit scores, minimum down payment, and debt-to-income ratios before they even open the door to the first model. Give the customer a chance to care about the home and become connected emotionally to the experience before you say that it's out of their price range, or smaller than they had in mind. Let the customer fall in love with the home's kitchen, the walk-in closets and the view from the patio before you talk about earnest money, application fees and construction changes. Those discussions will come, but pace yourself. A little sugar goes a long way. Don't scare your customer off on the first date.

think

Think of a time in the past when you tried to dish out medicine before giving the customer enough sugar. How did that affect your sales experience with that customer?

_____

_____

_____

_____

_____

D A R E

I dare you today to make a list of all the questions or statements that could be perceived as negative or stressful to the customer. Make a point of discussing those topics only after the customer has built an emotional connection to you, your homes, or your community.

_____

_____

_____

_____

_____

_____

_____

a little sugar goes a long way

reflect

1. Did you bring up anything negative or stressful prior to creating an emotional connection to you, your homes, or your community?
    Circle one: YES NO
    If Yes, what did you say?

    _____

    _____

    _____

2. How did that impact your experience with the customer?

    _____

    _____

    _____

    _____

    _____

    _____

3. What can you do in the future to be aware of how many emotionally negative and positive questions/statements you are communicating to your customers?

    _____

    _____

    _____

    _____

4. If you consistently execute this Dare with every prospect you see over the next year, how many sales would this Dare earn you? Circle one:

.25 sales .5 sales .75 sales 1 sale

1.25 sales 1.5 sales 1.75 sales 2 sales

effort

Rate your effort level towards improving yourself today with this Dare:

1 2 3 4 5 6 7 8 9 10

1: Did not read or do the Dare. 2: Read the Dare, but did not do it. 5: Did the Dare with half of my customers today. 10: Did the Dare with all customers today, and rehearsed the questions between customer encounters.

Dare 2

All She Wanted
Was a Little Black Dress

read

My wife knew just what she wanted to wear to the formal New Year's Eve party. It was a special night, so she was looking for a special dress. In her mind, she saw an elegant silk dress. It was black, strapless and cut above the knee. She went to several of her favorite department and specialty stores looking for *the* dress.

She never did find the perfect dress that she had created in her mind. Some dresses were just a bit too short; others were the right length, but had straps. So, did she buy a dress? Yes. She ended up with the one that was closest to what she wanted and within her budget. And in the end, she was very happy with it.

Your customer's vision is just the starting point, not the ending point. Don't kill yourself if you don't have exactly what they are looking for. Instead, focus on what you *do* have that is most similar to what they want. Your customers will end up buying the home that is closest to their needs, just like my wife's little black dress.

think

Think back to your last major purchase. In what ways was it different from what you first pictured?

23

My customer's vision is just the
starting point, not the ending point.

_____

_____

_____

_____

Were you still happy with your decision? Of course you were, or you would not have purchased the item. Your customers will be satisfied, too.

D A R E

Today I dare you to find out what the customer is looking for, and then use their vision as a starting point rather than an ending point. If you don't have exactly what the customer says they want, use the following question to uncover why they are looking for what they say they want:

"I am curious. What's important to you about that (size, layout, number of rooms, specific feature)?"

reflect

1. How did it remove pressure from you when you did not focus on having the perfect home for your customers?

_____

_____

_____

_____

_____

_____

_____

_____

_____

_____

2. How were you able to show homes to more of your customers by not having to eliminate ones that you did not think would interest them? (If you did not have any customers, then can you see how you might have eliminated customers in the past?)

_____

_____

_____

_____

_____

_____

_____

3. Do you have any success stories of a customer who ended up liking something different from what they initially said they wanted? (If you don't have an example from today, then write down an example of a past customer.)

_____

_____

_____

_____

_____

_____

_____

_____

_____

_____

_____

4. Do you see how there is no such thing as a perfect home and community? Why are customers' initial "wants" a moving target?

_____

_____

_____

_____

_____

_____

_____

5. If you consistently execute this Dare with every prospect you see over the next year, how many sales would this Dare earn you? Circle one:

.25 sales   .5 sales   .75 sales   1 sale

1.25 sales   1.5 sales   1.75 sales   2 sales

effort

Rate your effort level towards improving yourself today with this Dare:

1   2   3   4   5   6   7   8   9   10

1: Did not read or do the Dare. 2: Read the Dare, but did not do it. 5: Did the Dare with half of my customers today. 10: Did the Dare with all customers today, and rehearsed the questions between customer encounters.

"The sheer act of picking up the phone for an hour a week — every week — increases your sales."

Dare 3

Show Up

r e a d

Woody Allen, American film director, says, "Eighty percent of success is showing up." In sales, showing up physically *and* mentally automatically increases your chances for success.

"Showing up" in new home sales means consistently doing those daily tasks that often fall by the wayside: sweeping your entrance, changing burnt bulbs, and making those follow-up calls every week. We'll focus on that last one today.

If you've been in the business long enough, you already know that the sheer act of picking up the phone for an hour a week—every week—increases your sales. Even though it's tempting to feel like you've done all you can after your first two contacts with your prospect (their initial visit and the follow-up call you made within a week), research shows that prospects need eight to twelve contacts before they make a decision. If you have a competitive streak (and you're in sales, so you probably do), then think of it as a race between you and your competition—first one to twelve contacts wins!

By picking up the phone, you've already shown up physically, but there's a bit more to the story. Now it's time to show up mentally. The prevalence of e-mail, call waiting, and other forms of instant communication makes for a society of chronic multi-taskers, and you can tell when your spouse or friend is multi-tasking and disengaged from the conversation. Hint: your

29

customers can, too. Distractions are inevitable, but you can do your part by turning off your cell phone, closing your e-mail, and telling your coworkers that you are making follow-up calls and are not to be disturbed.

When you call your prospects, picture yourself sitting next to them. You wouldn't check your e-mail, surf the web, or play computer Solitaire if they were sitting beside you, so don't do it while you're on the phone. This allows you to focus intently on what they say and on how they say it. The customer *must* feel that you are tuning the world out and tuning in only them!

Listen to Woody Allen (he's a very successful fellow, after all) and show the heck up today.

t h i n k

Write down a 60-minute time slot for when you will make your follow-up calls. Place it in your calendar as a recurring appointment every week.

D A R E

I dare you today to call your prospects for one hour. Place enough prospects in front of you to fill up one hour's time. (Tip: You should have at least 25 prospects to compensate for non-answered calls.) If you go through all of your pre-determined calls before the 60 minutes are up, then call other prospects. Do not stop calling until 60 minutes are up.

picture myself sitting next to them

r e f l e c t

1. How many calls did you make today?

    _____

2. How many people did you speak to today?

    _____

3. How many appointments did you make today?

    _____

4. What percentage of the 60 minutes did you use to make your phone calls today?

    _____%

    Note: If the answer is 100%, then congratulate yourself for investing in your career and move on to Question 5. For anything less than 100%, consider why you didn't make the calls:

    a. Were you unprepared?

    b. Were you afraid that you were going to bother the prospect?

    c. Did you forget?

5. What did you learn about your customers by calling them? Write out a specific example.

    _____

    _____

    _____

_____

_____

_____

_____

_____

6. By making the calls, were you better equipped to accomplish your customers' goals and, in so doing, to improve their lives? How?

_____

_____

_____

_____

_____

_____

7. If you consistently execute this Dare with every prospect you see over the next year, how many sales would this Dare earn you? Circle one:

.25 sales   .5 sales   .75 sales   1 sale

1.25 sales   1.5 sales   1.75 sales   2 sales

effort

Rate your effort level towards improving yourself today with this Dare:

1   2   3   4   5   6   7   8   9   10

1: Did not read or do the Dare. 2: Read the Dare, but did not do it. 5: Did the Dare with half of my customers today. 10: Did the Dare with all customers today, and rehearsed the questions between customer encounters.

Dare 4

Plot a Course

r e a d

Imagine yourself and a wee companion (maybe your child, niece, or nephew) on a Disneyland tour. You're in search of hidden treasure, but along the way, there are rides to ride, magical worlds to explore and characters to meet. Your tour guide takes her time, pointing out each exciting feature along the way, and snapping photographs of the kids shaking hands with Mickey Mouse. However, she steers clear of a popular roller-coaster that is under repair at the moment. She takes great care in creating the best experience possible because she wants your young companion to remember meeting Mickey, not the disappointment of not being able to ride Gadget's Go Coaster.

Think of yourself as a Disneyland tour guide (minus the Mickey Mouse hat and the plaid skirt or vest), and remember that the path is as important as the destination. So consciously plan a route that allows you to stroll past the manicured lawns and the neighborhood parks rather than the dry brown lawns and cars propped up on blocks.

You and the Disneyland tour guide share a common mission: to create the best perception possible of your little corner of the world.

The path is as important as the destination.

think

Drive your community today, making note (with pen and paper, not just mentally) of all the features you'd like to highlight in your approach and departure, as well as those you'd like to avoid. Plot a course on your plat map that highlights the positive features and avoids the unsightly ones.

DARE

I dare you today to take every customer along your planned route and re-plan your course as your community changes.

reflect

1. Why do you believe you or other salespeople in the past have not given each customer the "Disneyland" tour of the community?

_____

_____

_____

_____

_____

_____

_____

_____

_____

2. What did you do differently in your tour today because of this Dare? If you're in an unfinished community, what did you do to help your customer envision a finished product?

_____

_____

_____

_____

_____

_____

_____

_____

_____

3. How did it improve their home search experience with you?

_____

_____

_____

_____

_____

_____

_____

_____

4. By touring your customers in this way, what did you learn about them or your community that you would not have known otherwise?

_____

_____

_____

_____

_____

_____

_____

_____

_____

5. If you consistently execute this Dare with every prospect you see over the next year, how many sales would this Dare earn you? Circle one:

.25 sales   .5 sales   .75 sales   1 sale

1.25 sales   1.5 sales   1.75 sales   2 sales

effort

Rate your effort level towards improving yourself today with this Dare:

1   2   3   4   5   6   7   8   9   10

1: Did not read or do the Dare. 2: Read the Dare, but did not do it. 5: Did the Dare with half of my customers today. 10: Did the Dare with all customers today, and rehearsed the questions between customer encounters.

Dare 5

Pick the Right Song

r e a d

Year after year, a few contestants on Fox's hit reality show *American Idol* hear one phrase from the judges: "Pick the right song." It's been the kiss of death for talented, hardworking and highly motivated contestants.

Remember Brooke White? Even vaguely? Though her voice was stellar, her name was lost in the unmemorable ghosts of *Idol's* past. How about Lil Rounds? Week after week, the judges dinged the 2009 contestant for choosing songs that weren't right for her unique style and voice. Contestants do best when they select songs that allow them to perform in their element.

These star contestants end up watching the final show from their couches. So what separates these hardworking vocalists from the final two *Idol* contestants? Picking the right song.

See, I think the same thing happens to salespeople. Sometimes talented, hardworking, and highly motivated salespeople end up lost in the mix of a customer's home search because the salesperson picks the wrong song. What does the wrong song mean for you as a salesperson? It means you present a solution to a customer's problem before you really understand what the customer is looking for. As a result, your "performance" misses the mark and falls flat. As a salesperson, you really have to understand your customer's unique needs *before* you start presenting the solution.

You can gain that understanding by finding out what's wrong with your customer's current home and community, why they are moving, and what you have to offer that will improve their lives.

In so doing, you stand out as a contestant who chose the right song, and it will make you more likely to get your customer's vote.

t h i n k

Think back to the last time you started selling before you really understood what the customer needed. Mentally retrace your steps through the interaction, from the moment you saw their car pull up to the time the client left. Is the picture coming back to you? Okay, what was one benefit or feature you "sold" before you truly knew what the client wanted? Now visualize the same car pulling up again, and walk through what you would do differently today.

_____

_____

_____

_____

D A R E

I dare you today to make it your goal to understand what the customer needs prior to showing your homes and community. You can accomplish this by asking the following three questions to every customer you meet:

- What is it about your current home that you want to change?

- What is it about your current community that you want to change?
- What's gotten you thinking about looking for something different?

Before the day starts, and between each customer, say the three questions aloud so that you memorize them and feel comfortable using them. Remember, the goal is to start showing or describing your homes only after you know that you have something that will specifically improve their life.

r e f l e c t

1. How did asking these three questions to your customers change your performance today, and how did it feel to use these questions?

_____

_____

_____

_____

_____

_____

2. With what percentage of your customers did you use all three questions?

_____%

Note: If the answer is 100%, then congratulate yourself for investing in your career, and move on to Question 3. For anything less than 100%, consider why you didn't ask each question to each customer:

a. Was it uncomfortable?

b. Were you afraid of the answer?

c. Did you forget?

39

3. What did you learn about your customers from using these questions?

_____

_____

_____

_____

_____

_____

4. Most importantly, did you hold off describing and showing your product until you knew that you had something that would improve the customer's life? Circle one: YES NO

   If Yes, how did that help you?

_____

_____

_____

_____

_____

_____

_____

5. If you consistently execute this Dare with every prospect you see over the next year, how many sales would this Dare earn you? Circle one:

   .25 sales   .5 sales   .75 sales   1 sale

   1.25 sales   1.5 sales   1.75 sales   2 sales

effort

Rate your effort level towards improving yourself today with this Dare:

1   2   3   4   5   6   7   8   9   10

1: Did not read or do the Dare. 2: Read the Dare, but did not do it. 5: Did the Dare with half of my customers today. 10: Did the Dare with all customers today, and rehearsed the questions between customer encounters.

I need to understand my customer's unique needs before I can present the solution.

Week 1
Day-Off Dares

"If you don't believe you can
be better, then there is no
motivation for you to labor for
your goals."

Believe in yourself.

Dare 6

Why Not?

read

Mia Michaels, Emmy Award-winning choreographer best known for her work on Fox TV's *So You Think You Can Dance*, has seen her pieces performed by Cirque du Soleil, Madonna, and Celine Dion, among others. When asked if it was intimidating to keep creating better dance routines, she said, "Absolutely! But as soon as it stops getting challenging to recreate and I get bored, then it's time to retire." Just think about that. It's a mindset that welcomes challenge and thrives on rising above circumstances. And it's a mindset that works.

The top politicians, leaders, businesspeople, dancers and musicians are not likely to get to the top by asking, "Why me?" or, "How could I possibly be the one to reach such a pinnacle?" If they don't believe they can be better, then there is no motivation to prepare and to labor for their goals. It's likely they won't go through the pain if they don't believe they can have the gain.

What would happen to your actions and behaviors if you started saying, "Why not?" rather than, "Of course not"? How would you approach your day differently if you responded to challenges not by asking, "Why?" but by asking, "How can I overcome this?"

think

How much do your beliefs affect what you do and think? Do you believe it's possible to do anything that is incongruent with your beliefs?

_____

_____

_____

_____

_____

_____

_____

_____

_____

DARE

Today I dare you to make two lists. Under "My competition believes…" write down all of the phrases you have said or heard people say in the past that caused you to doubt yourself and/or your ability to sell. Under "I believe…" write the beliefs you would like to adopt. Make three copies of these lists, and put a set in your bathroom, your office, and on your refrigerator. Starting today, read the "I believe" list aloud. Every time you or someone else says something from the "My competition believes" list, then consciously replace that phrase with one from your "I believe" list.

My competition believes...	I believe...

r e f l e c t

1. How would your sales results (or life) be different if all of your "I believe…" statements were true at this moment?

_____

_____

_____

_____

_____

_____

_____

_____

_____

2. If you consistently execute this Dare every day over the next year, how many sales would this Dare earn you? Circle one:

    .25 sales   .5 sales   .75 sales   1 sale

    1.25 sales   1.5 sales   1.75 sales   2 sales

e f f o r t

Rate your effort level towards improving yourself today with this Dare:

1   2   3   4   5   6   7   8   9   10

1: Did not read or do the Dare. 2: Read the Dare, but did not do it. 5: Did the Dare with half of my customers today. 10: Did the Dare with all customers today, and rehearsed the questions between customer encounters.

Dare 7

It's Not a Used Tissue!

r e a d

In my first book, *Creating Urgency in a Non-Urgent Housing Market*, I focused my writing around one main premise: **the desire to improve one's life has more influence over his or her buying decision than any other factor.** When this premise first struck me, I revered the thought and unveiled the line like a fine work of art. Since then, I've explained the concept before large audiences and on hundreds of coaching calls. On a recent sales visit of my own, I tossed the line out there as an afterthought. When my audience started scrambling to write it down, I realized that I had treated the line I once saw as a jewel more like a used tissue. The revelation was just as powerful to my audience as it had been to me when it first hit me. The line wasn't stale, but my delivery was.

This is a common pitfall in all performance-based careers. We confuse our perception with the customer's perception, and we neglect the very features that give us our edge. Your customers have never experienced what you see every day, so think about those unique qualities, special touches and hidden gems that set your community, your homes, and your builder apart. Remember these jewels and deliver the lines with the same reverence as you once did.

Is my delivery stale?

think

Do you revere the special features and qualities of your homes and community today, just as you did the first time you discovered them yourself? If so, do your actions reflect your beliefs?

_____

_____

_____

_____

DARE

I dare you to treat every customer this week as if it were the first time they had ever seen you, your product and your community. Speak about your home and community features as if it were your very first time to talk about them.

reflect

1. Write out some specific features of your home and community that you feel you need to present as "brand new" to your customers. What makes these features so special? Make sure you really believe they are special so you will present them that way.

_____

_____

_____

_____

_____

_____

_____

_____

_____

_____

_____

_____

2. How did renewing your perception about the special features in your home and community affect the way you interacted with customers this week?

_____

_____

_____

_____

_____

_____

_____

_____

_____

3. If you consistently take ownership over creating urgency with every prospect you see over the next year, how many sales would this Dare earn you? Circle one:

.25 sales   .5 sales   .75 sales   1 sale

1.25 sales   1.5 sales   1.75 sales   2 sales

e f f o r t

Rate your effort level towards improving yourself today with this Dare:

1   2   3   4   5   6   7   8   9   10

1: Did not read or do the Dare. 2: Read the Dare, but did not do it. 5: Did the Dare with half of my customers today. 10: Did the Dare with all customers today, and rehearsed the questions between customer encounters.

Week 1 Summary

Before you continue in your journey towards improvement, take a moment to get your bearings by completing your Week 1 Summary. **You must do this before you continue to Week 2.**

Average Effort Score for Week 1:

Review your Effort Scores from Dares 1-7, and calculate your Average Effort Score for the week. Write it in the space below.

_____

4 or less = It's time to get serious. Recommit yourself to the program, and start fresh in Week 2 by striving for a 5 or higher each day!

5 to 7 = You're off to a strong start, but you can do even better! Make a commitment today to raise the bar for yourself in Week 2, and strive for an average of 8 or better.

8 to 9 = What a great start! Keep pushing forward, and make it your personal goal to score all 9's and 10's in Week 2.

10 = Excellent! You are a rock star. If you maintain this effort level, you will receive the maximum benefit from this program, and you will achieve the success that you desire.

What's it worth?

What was this week worth to you? Flip back through Week 1, and tally the number of sales that you said Dares 1-7 would earn you. Write it below.

_____

7 Dares down... 33 to go!
You can do it!

53

Week 2

Dares 8-14

Day-On Dares

_____ 8.   Take Me Home with You

_____ 9.   Tell Me About Your Current Community

_____ 10. K.I.S.S.: Keep It Short and Simple

_____ 11. Move Them into the Home in Their Mind

_____ 12. You Can Handle the Truth

Day-Off Dares

_____ 13. You or Circumstance?

_____ 14. More Than Words

Remember: the desire to improve one's life has more influence over their buying decision than any other factor.

Dare 8

Take Me Home with You

read

What if you could go home with each of your customers? You could get inside their homes and walk through them room by room, discussing every pet peeve and every favorite feature about each space, and you'd be completely prepared to address their needs. When you open the kitchen cabinets and see a can of Raid next to the baby food, you'd know they need more storage. When you notice gardening tools in the laundry room, you'd know they need a bigger garage. No, I'm not trying to get you arrested here; so for our purposes, you'll have to settle for the next best thing, which is to have your customers mentally walk you through their homes. Ask questions like the following:

- Why did you choose your current home?
- What is your favorite room in your house?
- Where does each member of your family spend the most time?
- If you could change one thing about your kitchen, what would it be?

As you ask these questions (and don't pigeonhole yourself here, there are plenty more questions that give insight), your customer will have the opportunity to lay out all of the problems with their current home. That makes your job easy: offer solutions. If they just told you they need more storage, you can deliver that. People aren't going to argue with their own advice.

t h i n k

In what ways would it be easier to find the perfect home for someone if you were able to walk through their current home first?

_____

_____

_____

_____

offer solutions

D A R E

I dare you today to ask at least three of the following questions to every customer you see. When you don't have customers in front of you, practice saying them aloud.

- How long have you lived in your current home?
- How many homes did you look at before you chose your current home?
- Why did you choose your current home?
- What is your favorite room in the house?
- (If they are married.) What is your spouse's favorite room?
- (If they have children.) What are your children's favorite rooms?
- Which room does each family member spend the most time in?
- If you could change one thing about your kitchen, living room, dining room, entry, or master bedroom, what would it be?
- What additional spaces do you need in your next home?
- What spaces or rooms are you currently not using?
- Do you have enough storage in your home, or could you use more?

- Is your backyard the right size, or would you want it to be smaller or larger?

TIP: To prepare yourself for a stronger follow-up later, be sure to write your customer's answers on the back of their reg card.

reflect

1. Which three questions did you make a point to ask each customer today?

_____

_____

_____

_____

_____

_____

_____

_____

_____

2. How did asking these questions help you to tailor your sales presentation to your customers?

_____

_____

_____

_____

_____

_____

_____

_____

_____

_____

3. What will you do in the future to remind yourself to ask more questions about the customer's current home?

_____

_____

_____

_____

_____

_____

_____

_____

_____

4. If you consistently execute this Dare with every prospect you see over the next year, how many sales would this Dare earn you? Circle one:

    .25 sales   .5 sales   .75 sales   1 sale

    1.25 sales   1.5 sales   1.75 sales   2 sales

effort

Rate your effort level towards improving yourself today with this Dare:

1   2   3   4   5   6   7   8   9   10

1: Did not read or do the Dare. 2: Read the Dare, but did not do it. 5: Did the Dare with half of my customers today. 10: Did the Dare with all customers today, and rehearsed the questions between customer encounters.

"You are the catalyst for a customer's decision-making process."

— *Creating Urgency in a Non-Urgent Housing Market*

Dare 9

Tell Me About
Your Current Community

read

Yesterday (or on your last Day On), we talked about getting your customer to take you home with them. Now that you're nice and comfortable "going home" with your customer, we'll focus on something just as important. It's the same concept, but this time, you want them to walk you mentally through their community. The goal is to understand fully what they like and dislike about it. You'll ask questions regarding what amenities they have and what amenities they want; what they like about the location of their home and what they'd like to change; and what their surrounding neighborhood currently has or lacks.

Whether you're asking questions about their home or about their community, the goal is to position yourself to understand what your customer needs. This gives you a head start in the race to accomplish your customer's mission. Oh yes, this is a race. The salesperson who most quickly and completely understands the customer's mission, and then solves it the fastest, is the salesperson who wins the deal.

think

How will the customer's likes and dislikes concerning where they currently live influence their choice for the next community they will call home?

63

_____

_____

_____

_____

_____

_____

_____

DARE

I dare you today to ask at least three of the following questions to every customer you see. When you don't have customers in front of you, practice saying them aloud.

- How long have you lived in your current community?
- How many communities did you consider before you chose your current community?
- Besides the home itself, why did you choose your current community?
- (If they are married.) What is your spouse's favorite feature of your community?
- (If they have children.) What is your child's/children's favorite feature of your community?
- If you could change one thing about your community, what would it be?
- What features in your community are you not using?
- What features do you wish your current community had?

This is a race.

reflect

1. What did you learn about your customer's future community needs by asking questions about their current community likes and dislikes? (Be sure to note their answers on their information card to reference in your follow-up calls.)

_____

_____

_____

_____

_____

_____

_____

_____

2. How did asking those questions influence your sales presentation?

_____

_____

_____

_____

_____

_____

_____

3. If you consistently execute this Dare with every prospect you see over the next year, how many sales would this Dare earn you? Circle one:

    ```
    .25 sales    .5 sales    .75 sales    1 sale

    1.25 sales   1.5 sales   1.75 sales   2 sales
    ```

effort

Rate your effort level towards improving yourself today with this Dare:

```
1    2    3    4    5    6    7    8    9    10
```

1: Did not read or do the Dare. 2: Read the Dare, but did not do it. 5: Did the Dare with half of my customers today. 10: Did the Dare with all customers today, and rehearsed the questions between customer encounters.

Dare 10

K.I.S.S:
Keep It Short and Simple

read

"I have only made this letter rather long because I have not had time to make it shorter." — Blaise Pascal, 1662

Pascal, the French mathematician and philosopher, understood a concept many writers including Henry David Thoreau, T.S. Eliot, and Mark Twain have since echoed: the fewer the words, the better. Simplicity works both in writing and in follow-up calls because the more you talk, the less people remember.

After you've engaged your prospect on the phone, cut right to the chase and use the following three-step script:

- Summarize what you and the customer have accomplished so far,
- Tell them what comes next,
- And then set up an appointment to make it happen.

After you've summarized the accomplishments, the next step goes something like this:

"The next thing we need to do is go back through the two homes you liked and decide which one is a better fit for your family." Or, "The next thing I would like to do is cover our great financing options and show you how easy it is to buy a home." Or, "The next thing I would like to do is invite you to come out and play a match at our tennis courts."

Say what you need to say, schedule the next action and then get off the phone. Do what my editor tells me to do when she thinks I'm being long-winded: keep it short and simple (K.I.S.S).

think

Why do you and/or other salespeople cover too much detail over the phone instead of just cutting to the chase? How would it benefit you if you were in the customer's shoes and a salesperson used the three-step script?

_____

_____

_____

_____

D A R E

I dare you to call at least five prospects today. To prepare, write out your simple three-step script for each prospect prior to calling them. (Summarize what you and the customer have accomplished so far, tell them what comes next, and then set up an appointment to make it happen.)

reflect

1. How many of the five calls did you make today? _____ calls.
    Note: If the answer is all five, then congratulate yourself for investing in your career and move on to Question 2. If you made fewer than five calls, consider why you didn't make them:

a. Were you unprepared?

b. Were you afraid that you were going to bother the prospect?

c. Did you forget?

2. How did using the three-step script feel? Did it make your follow-up calls more productive?

_____

_____

_____

_____

_____

_____

_____

3. What did you learn about your customers by calling them?

_____

_____

_____

_____

_____

_____

_____

4. By making the calls and following the three-step script, were you better equipped to accomplish your customers' goals and, in so doing, to improve their lives?

_____

_____

_____

_____

_____

_____

_____

_____

5. If you consistently execute this Dare with every prospect you see over the next year, how many sales would this Dare earn you? Circle one:

.25 sales   .5 sales   .75 sales   1 sale

1.25 sales   1.5 sales   1.75 sales   2 sales

effort

Rate your effort level towards improving yourself today with this Dare:

1   2   3   4   5   6   7   8   9   10

1: Did not read or do the Dare. 2: Read the Dare, but did not do it. 5: Did the Dare with half of my customers today. 10: Did the Dare with all customers today, and rehearsed the questions between customer encounters.

Dare 11

Move Them into the Home in Their Mind

read

It was my first time meeting the "real" Mickey Mouse. I ate cotton candy, and my dad carried me around on his shoulders. I can almost hear "It's a Small World After All" as I write. It was my first visit to Disney World and the Epcot Center. I was eight.

How can I picture this image so vividly 23 years later, when I can't even remember where I park the car at the movie theater? Because emotions stick.

Buying a home is 85 percent emotional and only 15 percent logical. It's ranked as one of the top three most emotional and stress inducing life experiences—right up there with losing a loved one and divorce.

Get your customers to visualize what they'll do with each room, where their furniture will go, and who will be the first family they'll entertain on the porch. Start off by saying,

> "Let's go through the home together and talk about how you would use each room. This will help me understand how you will live in the space and help me find the best home for you."

At the front door, say,

> "I need you to tell me how the home feels as soon as you walk in. You and I both know that if it doesn't feel right as soon as you walk in, it probably isn't the home for you."

71

Then open the door, wait five seconds and ask how the home feels. If it's positive, continue through the home. If their first impressions are iffy, then ask why it doesn't feel quite right.

As you continue through the home say, "Okay, I want this to be interactive, so let's talk about each room." Walk the furniture off in the living room or sketch it on the floor plan at the end. The point is to have them moved into each room in their minds.

Succeed at that, and you're 85 percent there.

t h i n k

What are the first three things you think of when you hear the word "home?" *That's* what your clients are buying. They're purchasing a place to *live life*—not a concrete foundation, framed walls and insulated attic. With your next customer, how will you focus more on the lifestyle (where their furniture will fit and who they'll entertain) than on the nuts and bolts?

_____

_____

_____

_____

D A R E

I dare you today to focus on moving each customer into your homes emotionally. Memorize the above script and use it with each customer you speak to today. This script will get the customers primed for this activity. In between customer visits, rehearse the script and visualize moving the customer into your homes.

Emotions stick.

reflect

1. How did using the script feel? What can you do to feel more comfortable using it?

_____

_____

_____

_____

_____

_____

_____

2. With what percentage of your customers did you use the script?

_____%

Note: If the answer is 100%, then congratulate yourself for investing in your career and move on to Question 3. For anything less than 100%, consider why you didn't ask each question to each customer:

a. Was it uncomfortable?

b. Were you afraid of the answer?

c. Did you forget?

3. How did moving the customer into your homes emotionally work for you today? Explain.

_____

_____

_____

_____

_____

_____

_____

_____

_____

4. By focusing on moving your customers into the home emotionally, how were you able to create closer connections with them?

_____

_____

_____

_____

_____

_____

_____

_____

5. If you consistently execute this Dare with every prospect you see over the next year, how many sales would this Dare earn you? Circle one:

.25 sales   .5 sales   .75 sales   1 sale

1.25 sales   1.5 sales   1.75 sales   2 sales

effort

Rate your effort level towards improving yourself today with this Dare:

1   2   3   4   5   6   7   8   9   10

1: Did not read or do the Dare. 2: Read the Dare, but did not do it. 5: Did the Dare with half of my customers today. 10: Did the Dare with all customers today, and rehearsed the questions between customer encounters.

"... the objections your
prospects cite and their true
concerns are not always the
same thing."

Dare 12

You Can Handle the Truth

read

Objections are as much a part of your job as they are for any judge in a courtroom. For you, they're the reasons your customers don't want to move forward with their purchase. The trouble is that the objections your prospects cite and their true concerns are not always the same thing. Your challenge, then, is to seek out the true reason for each objection you hear today.

As a professional, it's your job to understand the real objection behind the spoken objection—don't just respond to the stated concern. This assures you maintain credibility with the prospect and earn their trust to continue with them on their home buying journey.

Picture the following scenario: You're talking to a customer—they're engaged in the discussion, you're in the rhythm, and you're feeling fine. Then, for some reason, they tell you that they're not so sure they want to live in your community after all. *They liked it five minutes ago*, you think, so you launch into all the reasons why your neighborhood is so perfect: the pool, the clubhouse, the great location. You've made a foolproof case, but then they utter the dreaded six words, "We need to think about it."

Why? Because you handled the wrong objection. You thought they did not like the overall community; that is, after all, what they seemed to be saying. However, that was not their true concern. If you'd have taken the time to dig a little deeper, you would have discovered that they do like your community; but they're concerned that the home you showed them is on a busy street. You did not seek the true concern, so you missed your opportunity to address it.

Today, whenever your prospects hesitate about your community, homes, or features, dig a little deeper and ask clarifying questions that help you uncover the real objection before you start defending your position.

The good news is that your prospects aren't on the stand in a courtroom, and they *want* you to know what they're looking for. So do them a favor, and ask them questions that help them communicate what they already want you to know.

That's right. You *can* handle the truth. And you must.

t h i n k

When was the last time you answered the spoken objection before seeking the true objection? Were you afraid of the customer's concern? Did you think you understood the objection, only to find out later that you didn't?

_____

_____

_____

_____

Conversely, think of an example of a time when you asked clarifying questions and discovered that the objections weren't as hard to address as you thought they were. If you've been selling on your own for a week, or

dig deeper and uncover their true concern

a decade, you've probably missed out on similar situations by not seeking the truth.

_____

_____

_____

_____

D A R E

I dare you today to seek the truth behind the objection. When you are talking to customers, I want you to seek the truth behind every objection you are given. Use clarifying questions such as, "Why are you concerned about x, y, and z?" and "What is it about the layout, size, location, etc., that bothers you?"

Don't just start talking without understanding the true objection. The best way to ensure that you have successfully sought the truth is to restate what you heard back to the customer. If you are right, or wrong, the customer will tell you.

reflect

1. How did you do on seeking the truth behind every objection? Explain.

_____

_____

_____

_____

2. Did you ask clarifying questions to understand the true objection?
    Circle one: YES NO

    If No, then why? If Yes, then write down the questions you used.

    _____

    _____

    _____

    _____

    _____

    _____

    _____

    _____

    _____

    _____

3. Write down how you restated a specific recent objection to ensure that
    you understood it.

    _____

    _____

    _____

    _____

    _____

    _____

4. Were you able to resolve the objection? Circle one: YES NO
   If not, then why?

   _____

   _____

   _____

   _____

   _____

   _____

5. If you consistently execute this Dare with every prospect you see over
   the next year, how many sales would this Dare earn you? Circle one:

   .25 sales   .5 sales   .75 sales   1 sale

   1.25 sales   1.5 sales   1.75 sales   2 sales

effort

Rate your effort level towards improving yourself today with this Dare:

1   2   3   4   5   6   7   8   9   10

1: Did not read or do the Dare. 2: Read the Dare, but did not do it. 5: Did the Dare with half of my customers today. 10: Did the Dare with all customers today, and rehearsed the questions between customer encounters.

Week 2
Day-Off Dares

"We cannot allow ourselves to be victims of circumstance."

— *Creating Urgency in a Non-Urgent Housing Market*

day off

Dare 13

You or Circumstance?

r e a d

In my years of training, coaching, and managing, I have never seen a salesperson performing perfectly and not selling. That's why I don't buy it when I hear salespeople say, "The market is tough. I just don't know what else to do," followed closely by, "I'm just too busy to do the sales training that you want me to do."

It does not make sense to complain about the outside circumstances affecting your success, and then say there is not enough time to improve your skills. The next time you start to complain about the market, your location, or the models you have, think instead about your performance and what you can *do* to overcome those circumstances. What training can you take? What book can you read? What person can you learn from? Once you invest 100 percent in your improvement, see what happens to your sales.

t h i n k

Why do you believe you (or other salespeople you know) have said there isn't enough time to train (or you don't need additional training because you're as good as you need to be), while also complaining that you are not selling as much as you need to sell?

_____

_____

_____

D A R E

I dare you today to reflect back on what you have said and thought since you first opened this book. Have you said that you don't have time to do the Dares, and at the same time complained that you are not selling as much as you need to? I dare you to put 100% effort into every Dare from this day forward.

r e f l e c t

1. What can you do to hold yourself accountable to focusing first on a perfect sales presentation, before complaining that it is impossible to sell more in your circumstances?

_____

_____

_____

_____

_____

_____

_____

_____

2. Why is it harder to focus on improving your own effort and execution of your sales presentation, than it is to stop complaining about the circumstances affecting your success?

_____

_____

_____

_____

_____

_____

_____

_____

3. If you consistently execute this Dare every day, and focus on your effort and self improvement, rather than on your circumstances, how many sales would this Dare earn you over the next year? Circle one:

.25 sales   .5 sales   .75 sales   1 sale

1.25 sales   1.5 sales   1.75 sales   2 sales

effort

Rate your effort level towards improving yourself today with this Dare:

1   2   3   4   5   6   7   8   9   10

1: Did not read or do the Dare. 2: Read the Dare, but did not do it. 5: Did the Dare with half of my customers today. 10: Did the Dare with all customers today, and rehearsed the questions between customer encounters.

"It's not just what you say, but <u>how</u> you say it that counts."

Dare 14

More Than Words

read

Your prospect's eyes light up when you show her the kitchen of her dreams. What's more, today only, you have special pricing for new clients. You're in sales, so this is where you earn your keep. You must instill a sense of urgency in your buyer. She needs to truly understand, not just hear, that if she walks away, she'll miss a great opportunity. She'll lose the game.

It's a strong message, and you're going to need a lot more than words to deliver it. According to Albert Mehrabian, Psychology professor at UCLA, the combination of your tone of voice and body language account for 93 percent of the listener's interpretation of your message. That's thirteen times more influential than the actual words you say. Your words only account for 7 percent of how your message is received. Lesson learned? It's not just what you say, but *how* you say it that counts.

As Pete Townshend, guitarist and songwriter for the band The Who, says, "It's the singer, not the song that makes the music move along." Your home and your community are the song, but no matter how lovely the words, it's you, the singer, who must bring the tune to life.

How can I bring my message to life?

89

t h i n k

Do you believe that 93 percent of how people interpret your message is based upon everything but the actual words you say? Why? Give an example of being "misinterpreted."

_____

_____

_____

_____

D A R E

I dare you this week to focus your attention on your tone of voice and body language in your sales presentations. In between customer visits, practice by saying aloud "The reason people choose us is…" Record yourself and play it back. Do you sound enthusiastic? Is the message believable? Ask your friends and family how you sound to them.

r e f l e c t

1. What did your friends and family say when you asked them if you sound enthusiastic and passionate when you talk about your community and homes?

_____

_____

_____

_____

_____

_____

2. Name three people you feel are persuasive because of their tone of
   voice and body language.

_____

_____

_____

_____

_____

3. How does their method compare to how you communicate?

_____

_____

_____

_____

_____

_____

_____

_____

_____

4. How did you communicate your message today to your customers?

_____

_____

_____

_____

5. How do you feel it impacted your message to your customers?

_____

_____

_____

_____

6. What can you do in the future to remind yourself to focus on your tone of voice and body language in your communication with others?

_____

_____

_____

_____

_____

7. If you consistently execute this Dare with every prospect you see over the next year, how many sales would this Dare earn you? Circle one:

    .25 sales   .5 sales   .75 sales   1 sale

    1.25 sales   1.5 sales   1.75 sales   2 sales

effort

Rate your effort level towards improving yourself today with this Dare:

1   2   3   4   5   6   7   8   9   10

1: Did not read or do the Dare. 2: Read the Dare, but did not do it. 5: Did the Dare with half of my customers today. 10: Did the Dare with all customers today, and rehearsed the questions between customer encounters.

Pause here!

Week 2 Summary

Before you continue in your journey towards improvement, take a moment to get your bearings by completing your Week 2 Summary. **You must do this before you continue to Week 3.**

Average Effort Score for Week 2:

Review your Effort Scores from Dares 8-14, and calculate your Average Effort Score for the week. Write it in the space below.

_____

4 or less = It's time to get serious. Recommit yourself to the program, and start fresh in Week 3 by striving for a 5 or higher each day!

5 to 7 = You're doing well, but you can do even better! Make a commitment today to raise the bar for yourself in Week 3, and strive for an average of 8 or better.

8 to 9 = What a great week! Keep pushing forward, and make it your personal goal to score all 9's and 10's in Week 3.

10 = Excellent! You are a rock star. If you maintain this effort level, you will receive the maximum benefit from this program, and you will achieve the success that you desire.

What's it worth?

What was this week worth to you? Flip back through Week 2, and tally the number of sales that you said Dares 8-14 would earn you. Write it below.

_____

14 Dares down... 26 to go!
You can do it!

Week 3

Dares 15-21

Day-On Dares

_____ 15. Just Because You're Thinking It Doesn't Mean You've Accomplished It

_____ 16. Gambling is Prohibited on the Premises

_____ 17. Start with a Purpose

_____ 18. Get Ahead of the Pack

_____ 19. One Simple Close

Day-Off Dares

_____ 20. What Drives You?

_____ 21. Focus on the "Just Looking" Buyer

"Selling is all about decisions."

— *Leadership Selling*®

Dare 15

Just Because You're Thinking It Doesn't Mean You've Accomplished It

r e a d

A mutual accomplishment occurs when two things happen—you succeed in creating urgency in your customer, **and** your customer makes an emotional commitment through verbal agreement. That verbal part is important. Mutual accomplishment cannot be achieved with just a nod of the head. The best way to secure such an agreement is to ask a solid closing question that allows the customer to eliminate all other choices in their mind and make a final decision.

While you may feel that you have created urgency, it's not a mutual accomplishment until you've secured outward agreement from the customer. Julie helped demonstrate this point on one of our coaching calls. She was convinced that a customer was 100% in the bag, but couldn't tell me why except that they said they liked her home. I pushed a little more and asked why they liked hers more than the competition's. She still didn't know, so I asked Julie if it was possible that the customer told the competition the same thing. She admitted that was a possibility and recounted times when prospects told her they liked her home and then ended up buying from someone else. What Julie needed to do was remove all the guesswork by asking mutual accomplishment questions.

An example of a mutual accomplishment question is:

"You said that of all the homes that I showed you, the Dakota Plan was the best fit for you. Before you started looking in this community, you said that the Colorado Plan over at XYZ Homes was your favorite. Between the Dakota and Colorado, which one is better suited for your family's next home?"

If the customer says the Dakota (your home), then say, "I am always curious how my customers end up choosing their favorite home. So tell me, why do you feel the Dakota is a better fit?" On the other hand, if they tell you the Colorado is still their favorite, then ask why and see if you can find a better home in your inventory.

The purpose of a mutual accomplishment question is to bring verbal resolution to the major decisions in their home purchase. Remember, this is something you are doing *for* your customers, not *to* them. It helps them move forward in finding the best home, and helps you eliminate guesswork.

Note: For further study on this topic, refer to Chapter 5 in my book *Creating Urgency in a Non-Urgent Housing Market*.

t h i n k

What is your biggest fear about asking the mutual accomplishment questions in the above script?

_____

_____

_____

_____

_____

This is something I do for my customers, not to them.

_____

_____

_____

D A R E

I dare you to ask the mutual accomplishment question below to every customer you see today. Practice the question aloud between customer visits to increase your comfort.

"You said that of all the homes that I showed you, our _____ plan was the best fit for you. Before you started looking in this community, you said that the _(competitor's plan)_ over at _(competitor's community)_ was your favorite. Between these two plans, which one is better suited for your family's next home?"

reflect

1. Write out one example of a customer who you thought liked your home, but ended up buying from the competition.

_____

_____

_____

_____

_____

_____

2. Write out one example of a customer you practiced this Dare on today. Write the exact wording of your mutual accomplishment question as well as the customer's response.

_____

_____

_____

_____

_____

_____

_____

_____

_____

3. How will asking mutual accomplishment questions help you carry out the customer's mission of finding the best home for them?

_____

_____

_____

_____

_____

_____

_____

4. If you consistently execute this Dare with every prospect you see over the next year, how many sales would this Dare earn you? Circle one:

```
.25 sales    .5 sales    .75 sales    1 sale

1.25 sales   1.5 sales   1.75 sales   2 sales
```

effort

Rate your effort level towards improving yourself today with this Dare:

```
1   2   3   4   5   6   7   8   9   10
```

1: Did not read or do the Dare. 2: Read the Dare, but did not do it. 5: Did the Dare with half of my customers today. 10: Did the Dare with all customers today, and rehearsed the questions between customer encounters.

"... when it comes to building emotional urgency, your goal is to help the customer make a decision with confidence."

— *Creating Urgency in a Non-Urgent Housing Market*

Dare 16

Gambling is Prohibited
on the Premises

r e a d

It's notoriously difficult to find a good stylist for curly hair, and my wife has some seriously curly hair. Shelly usually wears her brown curls long, but wanted to change it up a bit and have it cut just above the shoulders. She went to a new salon, met her hairdresser, and told her what she wanted. The hairdresser listened, said, "No problem," and started cutting away. Minutes into the cut, Shelly got nervous—it was much shorter than she had described. She told the stylist, but by this point, Shelly already had a pile of curly hair at her feet. Starting the cut before she understood what Shelly wanted was quite a gamble on the hairdresser's part. Shelly's confidence in the stylist faded fast, and the next half-hour was awkward and quiet for both of them.

Though her hair ended up looking fine, Shelly left with zero faith in the stylist, and you had better believe she didn't go back.

All the hairdresser needed to do was summarize Shelly's vision back to her. This would have given the stylist the chance to make absolutely sure she understood Shelly's desired haircut, or to have Shelly clarify if necessary. Shelly would have had confidence in the leadership of the hairstylist, and the stylist would have been sure that she was giving Shelly what she wanted.

In the same way, when a customer comes to look at your homes, you must find out the general concept of what they are looking for and then summarize it back to them. This will increase your credibility with the customer, and it will give you confidence in the direction you should travel with them.

Save your gambling for the casino, not the sales office.

t h i n k

Why is it that people in sales positions, from those waiting tables to those selling homes, neglect to summarize back to the customer what the customer wants? Is it because of fear? Is it because they feel it's not necessary? How many communication blunders would be prevented if people would just restate what they heard a person say?

_____

_____

_____

_____

_____

D A R E

I dare you today to really listen to what the customer is looking for in their next home and community. Once you understand what their vision of their new home is, summarize it back to them. Do not begin showing them a home until you can do this.

Summarize the customer's vision back to them.

reflect

1. How did you do with listening to the customer well enough to be able to summarize what they wanted? Explain.

   _____

   _____

   _____

   _____

   _____

   _____

   _____

2. Did you summarize the customer's vision back to every customer you met today? If not, then why not?

   _____

   _____

   _____

   _____

   _____

   _____

   _____

   _____

3. How did summarizing the vision of the home affect the demonstration? Did you find your sales process more purposeful?

_____

_____

_____

_____

_____

_____

_____

4. How did summarizing the vision of the home affect your confidence in your solution for the customer?

_____

_____

_____

_____

_____

_____

_____

5. If you consistently execute this Dare with every prospect you see over the next year, how many sales would this Dare earn you? Circle one:

    .25 sales   .5 sales   .75 sales   1 sale

    1.25 sales   1.5 sales   1.75 sales   2 sales

e f f o r t

Rate your effort level towards improving yourself today with this Dare:

1   2   3   4   5   6   7   8   9   10

1: Did not read or do the Dare. 2: Read the Dare, but did not do it. 5: Did the Dare with half of my customers today. 10: Did the Dare with all customers today, and rehearsed the questions between customer encounters.

No one knows the homebuying
journey better than you do.

Dare 17

Start with a Purpose

r e a d

My tailor has a way of guiding me through the alteration process and assuring me that my suits are in good hands. He'll say things like, "Since you'd like the pant legs to fall a little higher on your shoes, I'm going to take the inseams in a little here." It's his way of letting me know he's heard me, and that he knows how to achieve my desired result. I leave feeling confident that I'm going to get a suit that fits just right.

As a salesperson, you're like that skilled tailor. No one knows the process, the end result, and the homebuying journey better than you do. You have to convey this confidence to your customers so they know where you are taking them, why you are leading in a specific direction, and how you will reach a successful end of the journey. You do this by giving the customer a ***purposeful transition statement***—it tells the buyer where you're heading, and *why* you're going there. For you, the conversation might go like this:

> "Based on your desire for four bedrooms and a kitchen island, we'll start with the second model. As we walk through the home, we'll talk about what's important to you in each room, and by the end, I'll use everything you've told me to take you to the best home for your needs."

109

Like the tailor, you're assuring your customer that you heard their needs and know best how to meet them.

t h i n k

What will it say to the customer about you when you start off the sales presentation with a purposeful transition statement?

_____

_____

_____

_____

D A R E

I dare you today to start off every sales presentation with a purposeful transition statement. Use the following template to help you, if you'd like.

"Based on your desire for _____, we'll start with the _____ model. As we walk through the home, we'll talk about what's important to you in each room, and by the end, I'll use everything you've told me to take you to the best home for your needs."

r e f l e c t

1. What happened to your sales presentations today when you started off with a purposeful transition statement?

110

_____

_____

_____

_____

_____

_____

_____

_____

_____

2. How did it impact your confidence in taking the customer to the home in your community that best meets their needs?

_____

_____

_____

_____

_____

_____

_____

_____

3. If you consistently execute this Dare with every prospect you see over the next year, how many sales would this Dare earn you? Circle one:

```
.25 sales    .5 sales    .75 sales    1 sale

1.25 sales   1.5 sales   1.75 sales   2 sales
```

effort

Rate your effort level towards improving yourself today with this Dare:

```
1   2   3   4   5   6   7   8   9   10
```

1: Did not read or do the Dare. 2: Read the Dare, but did not do it. 5: Did the Dare with half of my customers today. 10: Did the Dare with all customers today, and rehearsed the questions between customer encounters.

Dare 18

Get Ahead of the Pack

r e a d

1. How long have you been looking for a home?
2. How many homes (including resale) have you seen?
3. If you had to choose a home today, which one would it be?
4. Why is that your favorite home so far?
5. What, if anything, is the home lacking that you were hoping to find?

Picture yourself at the start of a five-leg relay race. Your palms are sweaty, your mouth is dry, and every muscle in your body is anticipating the familiar crack of the starting gun. Your competitors are lined up in the lanes to either side of you. They're ready, too. Now consider the five legs to be the five major factors that influence your customer's final decision: best home, best time frame, best price, best community, and best location.

What would happen if you could start the race at the third leg while the other runners started at the first? You guessed it—you'd win the race! By asking the five simple questions listed at the beginning of this Dare, you will uncover what matters most to your buyer, and you will zoom ahead of the pack. Now all you need to do is *listen* to their needs and find the home that has, not just everything they love, but everything they haven't been able to find, yet. It's a win/win. They get *the* home they've been looking for, you get the sale, and together you both cross the finish line. Everyone wins—except your competitors.

think

List the top three reasons you might resist (or have resisted) asking these questions. When you have your three reasons, consider this foolproof truth: knowing what your clients want is *always* better than not knowing, even if it's tough to hear. When you know the problem, you can work towards a solution.

_____

_____

_____

_____

DARE

I dare you today to focus on asking the five questions listed above within the first five minutes of meeting a new customer. Heck, try it with your old ones, too! Before the day starts and between each customer, say the five questions aloud so that you memorize them and feel comfortable using them.

reflect

1. How did using these questions feel? Explain.

_____

_____

If I uncover what matters most to my buyer, I will zoom ahead of the pack.

_____

_____

_____

_____

2. With what percentage of your customers did you use all five questions?

_____%

Note: If the answer is 100%, then congratulate yourself for investing in your career and move on to Question 3. For anything less than 100%, consider why you didn't ask each question to each customer:

a. Was it uncomfortable?

b. Were you afraid of the answer?

c. Did you forget?

3. What did you learn about your customers from using these questions?

_____

_____

_____

_____

_____

_____

_____

_____

_____

4. By asking these questions, were you better equipped to accomplish your customers' goals and, in so doing, to improve their lives? Explain.

_____

_____

_____

_____

_____

_____

_____

_____

_____

_____

5. If you consistently execute this Dare with every prospect you see over the next year, how many sales would this Dare earn you? Circle one:

.25 sales   .5 sales   .75 sales   1 sale

1.25 sales   1.5 sales   1.75 sales   2 sales

effort

Rate your effort level towards improving yourself today with this Dare:

1   2   3   4   5   6   7   8   9   10

1: Did not read or do the Dare. 2: Read the Dare, but did not do it. 5: Did the Dare with half of my customers today. 10: Did the Dare with all customers today, and rehearsed the questions between customer encounters.

Dare 19

One Simple Close

r e a d

You won't need the mountains of books on how to close a deal if you can master just one technique. The most natural and effective tool I've found is the *summary close*, which leads into the *transaction close*. Check out the following salesperson summary:

"When we first started looking for your next home, you said you were looking for a place with four bedrooms, two-and-a-half baths, a game room and a study. You mentioned that you needed the study to be located away from the main living area, and that you wanted a backyard that gave your children enough space to play. While we were looking at houses, you realized that you would enjoy a larger kitchen with more cabinet space, and a large bar area where your children could do homework while you made dinner. I showed you the Huntington floor plan, the Meredith, and the Richmond, and you agreed that the Richmond best fit what you were looking for in a home. I also showed you home sites on which to build the Richmond plan, and 2616 Waters Edge Lane was your favorite. Well, Mr. and Mrs. Prospect, the next thing left for us to do is to get the paperwork started and write a deposit so that we can make that home site yours! Are you ready to get started?"

Selling breaks down into three stages:

1. Understand the customer's mission,

2. Solve the customer's mission,

3. And hold the customer accountable to achieving their mission.

As in the scenario above, you summarize the first two stages (summary close), which sets you up to ask for the third stage (transaction close). Summarizing allows the customer to remember what they initially said they needed, and then to agree that they made the decisions necessary to accomplish those needs. You keep the decision-making process moving forward by asking them to commit to the next step: the paperwork and deposit.

Now that you've seen how a summary close leads naturally to a transaction close, it's time for you to practice using this strategy!

t h i n k

Do you believe the closing step is something you do to someone or for someone? How does that belief affect your attitude and behaviors towards asking a final close question?

_____

_____

_____

D A R E

I dare you today to use the summary close followed by the transaction close with every customer you talk to today. Practice between customer visits to increase your comfort and confidence with this new technique.

summary close → transaction close

reflect

1. What happened when you used the summary close followed by the transaction close today? Explain.

_____

_____

_____

_____

_____

_____

_____

2. Regardless of whether the customer said Yes or No, how did it feel using that closing strategy? Did it feel comfortable and natural? If not, then why not?

_____

_____

_____

_____

_____

_____

_____

3. Did summarizing for the customer what you accomplished, in regard to what they admittedly wanted, give you the confidence you needed to ask them to make the final purchase decision?

_____

_____

_____

_____

_____

_____

_____

_____

_____

4. If you consistently execute this Dare with every prospect you see over the next year, how many sales would this Dare earn you? Circle one:

   .25 sales   .5 sales   .75 sales   1 sale

   1.25 sales   1.5 sales   1.75 sales   2 sales

effort

Rate your effort level towards improving yourself today with this Dare:

1   2   3   4   5   6   7   8   9   10

1: Did not read or do the Dare. 2: Read the Dare, but did not do it. 5: Did the Dare with half of my customers today. 10: Did the Dare with all customers today, and rehearsed the questions between customer encounters.

Week 3
Day-Off Dares

"... your desire to improve your <u>own</u> <u>life</u> has more influence over your success than any other factor."

———

"You have to change <u>why</u> you sell <u>before</u> you can change <u>how</u> you sell."

— *Creating Urgency in a Non-Urgent Housing Market*

Dare 20

What Drives You?

r e a d

People say I look like him, walk like him, and talk like him; but I got more from my dad than just looks. I got his independence and drive. So when I was in high school, I asked him what career he'd recommend that would give me the most ownership over my results. I wanted to know that the harder I tried, the more I'd be rewarded. He advised me to go into commission sales and explained that salespeople drive revenue for the entire company. Without them (without you), companies can't pay for any other staff member. Great salespeople are in demand in every industry, in every city, and in every economy.

So let me ask you, why are you doing this? Why do you pound the pavement each day, work long, unpredictable hours and live a different life-style than the 9-to-5ers? If your first thought was "to make money," then I challenge you to go a little deeper. What can the money bring you? Will it allow you to buy a home or car you've always desired? Will it help pay for your kid's college education? Will it bring you a better life?

Remember, the biggest advantage to being a salesperson is that you don't have to be dependent upon a certain salary. Yes, it's true that you risk making less than a salary-based job, but with greater risk, there's also a potential for greater reward.

So, what's your motivation? Humans are more emotional beings than they are logical beings. If you can tap into your emotional motivations and answer the questions in today's dare, you will be more successful.

think

Why did you choose a career in sales? Did you think it would be easy to make a lot of money, or were you excited that the harder you worked, the more money you'd make? In what ways has the career met or exceeded your expectations so far?

_____

_____

_____

_____

_____

D A R E

I dare you today to take honest inventory of your motivations in the next section. How you answer these questions will impact how successful you can become.

reflect

1. What is your emotional motivation behind choosing a career in commission sales?

124

WHAT'S MY MOTIVATION?

_____
_____
_____
_____
_____
_____
_____

2. How much money do you make per house you sell? (Don't even think about writing a percent; you can't pay your mortgage with a percent.)

_____

3. How many houses do you need to sell each month to pay for your basic needs?

_____

4. How many houses do you need to sell each month to pay for your wants?

_____

5. How are you going to spend the money that you make above your needs? The more detail you write, the more you will mentally own this!

_____
_____
_____
_____

125

_____
_____
_____
_____
_____
_____
_____
_____
_____
_____
_____
_____

6. If you consistently focus on what money can do for you and your family, versus just working to sell a house, how many sales would this Dare earn you over the next year? Circle one:

    .25 sales   .5 sales   .75 sales   1 sale

    1.25 sales   1.5 sales   1.75 sales   2 sales

effort

Rate your effort level towards improving yourself today with this Dare:

1   2   3   4   5   6   7   8   9   10

1: Did not read or do the Dare. 2: Read the Dare, but did not do it. 5: Did the Dare with half of my customers today. 10: Did the Dare with all customers today, and rehearsed the questions between customer encounters.

126

Dare 21

Focus on the "Just Looking" Buyer

read

There are two types of buyers that walk into your sales office: those who admit to being buyers ("I'm looking for a three-bedroom…") and those who don't ("I just wanted to get some decorating ideas"). I need you to focus on the second kind today.

Yes, I know. The cold, distant, closed-off customers are harder to sell to, but I want you to see every "just-looking, not-interested" buyer as a fun challenge. See how far you can take them in the sales process. Can you get them talking about their current home? Can you get them talking about the other homes that they are "just looking" at? Can you get them to picture their furniture in your model's living room? It's not so much about selling them a home, but about getting them to open up to you.

Remember that your distant little Looky Lous are sometimes actually buyers who just don't know what they don't know. They're not even sure if they need a new home, and they certainly don't want to admit to themselves or to you that they're considering one. Nevertheless, something compelled them to start looking; they did come into your sales office, right?

By seeing each of these buyers as a challenge, you're making a way for yourself to become a better salesperson with all of your prospects, and you just might find a Looky Lou who wasn't "just looking," after all.

need to see how far I can take them in the sales process

127

remember: something compelled them to come here

think

Write down a purchase that you have made in the past that started with an "I'm just looking" attitude. What made you go from "just looking" to signing on the dotted line?

_____

_____

_____

_____

DARE

I dare you this week to focus on the "just looking" buyers. Slow down and see how far you can take them in the sales process. Use any of the previous Dares to help. Don't worry about selling them a home, just get them talking about their dissatisfaction.

reflect

1. Why are you so afraid of the "just looking" buyer? If you engage them, what's the worst thing that could happen? Explain.

_____

_____

_____

_____

_____

2. How did your perception of "just looking" buyers change as you found out more about their dissatisfaction with their current situation?

_____

_____

_____

_____

_____

_____

3. What did you learn about yourself this week?

_____

_____

_____

_____

_____

_____

4. Write an example of how far you took a "just-looking" buyer in the sales process this week. What did you do to get them to open up? Is there anything that you could have done to take the customer even further? If so, what?

_____

_____

_____

_____

_____

_____

_____

_____

_____

_____

5. If you consistently execute this Dare with every closed-off prospect you see over the next year, how many sales would the strategy earn you? Circle one:

.25 sales   .5 sales   .75 sales   1 sale

1.25 sales   1.5 sales   1.75 sales   2 sales

effort

Rate your effort level towards improving yourself today with this Dare:

1   2   3   4   5   6   7   8   9   10

1: Did not read or do the Dare. 2: Read the Dare, but did not do it. 5: Did the Dare with half of my customers today. 10: Did the Dare with all customers today, and rehearsed the questions between customer encounters.

Week 3 Summary

Before you continue in your journey towards improvement, take a moment to get your bearings by completing your Week 3 Summary. **You must do this before you continue to Week 4.**

Average Effort Score for Week 3:

Review your Effort Scores from Dares 15-21, and calculate your Average Effort Score for the week. Write it in the space below.

_____

4 or less = It's time to get serious. Recommit yourself to the program, and start fresh in Week 4 by striving for a 5 or higher each day!

5 to 7 = You're doing well, but you can do even better! Make a commitment today to raise the bar for yourself in Week 4, and strive for an average of 8 or better.

8 to 9 = What a great week! Keep pushing forward, and make it your personal goal to score all 9's and 10's in Week 4.

10 = Excellent! You are a rock star. If you maintain this effort level, you will receive the maximum benefit from this program, and you will achieve the success that you desire.

What's it worth?

What was this week worth to you? Flip back through Week 3, and tally the number of sales that you said Dares 15-21 would earn you. Write it below.

_____

21 Dares down... 19 to go!
You can do it!

Week 4

Dares 22-28

Day-On Dares

_____ 22. The Unsellable Floor Plan

_____ 23. "Let's Go Back to the Office"

_____ 24. Create an Experience

_____ 25. People Can't Argue Emotion, Only Logic

_____ 26. Three Simple Phrases

Day-Off Dares

_____ 27. Don't Wait for Urgency—Create It

_____ 28. Spend the Time

"People are buying homes in today's market. The only question is, whom are they buying homes from?"

— *Creating Urgency in a Non-Urgent Housing Market*

Dare 22

The Unsellable Floor Plan

read

Several years ago, I analyzed two communities with wildly different sales results for the same floor plan. At one community, the plan simply wouldn't sell; but just 15 miles away, the same home was the top seller. Since buyer demographics, prices, and incentives were comparable in both neighborhoods, I went looking for the variable.

After a brief discussion with the salesperson at each location, I discovered the problem. The salesperson at the first community hated the layout and couldn't understand why anyone would want to buy this plan. However, in the second community, the salesperson adored the plan and said that every customer he showed it to fell in love with the home. So what made the plan "unsellable" in the first community? The salesperson did. Scary, huh?

Whether you love or hate a floor plan, you have to realize that it was designed specifically for *somebody*. By the time the plan reaches your community, it's already been through the ringer with hours of review and architectural tweaks based on customer surveys, previous models, and research. Builders know better than to throw a poor plan out there and hope it works.

So get over yourself. Unless you're the one buying the home, it doesn't matter what you think. You're not going to live in it. Discover what's best for your customers, and you'll find that indeed, the plan you think is unsel-labe is the plan someone else wants to call home.

t h i n k

How much are you letting your opinions about a particular floor plan influence your message to your customers?

_____

_____

_____

_____

_____

D A R E

I dare you today to discover every hidden treasure about your least favorite floor plan. Ask sales managers and architects whom they had in mind when they designed the home. What niche were they trying to fill? Call a previous buyer and ask what their favorite feature was in the plan. Find out what the home has that other plans lack.

Now, rewrite their answers into selling statements such as, "When the architects designed this home, they had _____ in mind." Or, "People who chose this floor plan were looking for…." Choose one of your selling statements, and share it with every client you show the home to today.

r e f l e c t

1. What did you discover about your least favorite floor plan today that you did not previously know?

_____

_____

_____

_____

_____

_____

2. Were you able to share your statements of why people choose that floor plan with a customer today? If so, what happened?

_____

_____

_____

_____

_____

_____

_____

3. How did creating the selling statement for your least favorite floor plan change your opinion about that floor plan?

_____

_____

_____

_____

_____

_____

_____

4. What can you do in the future to not let your opinion get in the way of what is best for the customer?

_____

_____

_____

_____

_____

_____

_____

_____

5. If you consistently execute this Dare with every prospect you see over the next year, how many sales would this Dare earn you? Circle one:

    .25 sales   .5 sales   .75 sales   1 sale

    1.25 sales   1.5 sales   1.75 sales   2 sales

effort

Rate your effort level towards improving yourself today with this Dare:

1   2   3   4   5   6   7   8   9   10

1: Did not read or do the Dare. 2: Read the Dare, but did not do it. 5: Did the Dare with half of my customers today. 10: Did the Dare with all customers today, and rehearsed the questions between customer encounters.

"There are two types of
salespeople: those who
participate in the sales
process, and those who
influence the sales process."

— *Creating Urgency in a Non-Urgent Housing Market*

Dare 23

"Let's Go Back to the Office"

read

There are many techniques to get a customer back into your office at the end of a sales presentation, but there are fewer techniques simpler than just telling them. My mother, a professor of speech says, "Keep communication simple—tell people what you are going to tell them, tell them, and then tell them what you've told them."

So tell your customer up-front what to expect and how the process will go. You can say,

> "We're going to have a fun time together today. As we go through the homes and community, I'll take notes on things that you like. Before you leave, we'll go back to the office and I will create a packet for you that summarizes everything we've seen today and what we've accomplished so far."

I want to encourage you to set this expectation as early as possible because, the longer you wait, the more likely you are to chicken out.

Now let's fast-forward. You start out by telling them what to expect, you walk them through the models, and you take notes. When you're ready to take your customers back to the office, just lead the process by saying,

> "The next thing for us to do is head back to the office so I can create a customized packet just for you. I can also look up the information on

Set expectations as early as possible

141

option pricing you were wondering about, and write everything down for you."

Once they're in the sales office, summarize what you accomplished for them and answer any questions they have.

I'm going to take some poetic license here and add a little something to Mom's advice: tell them what you're going to tell them, tell them, tell them what you've told them... and then ask them to purchase from you.

t h i n k

Why will you be more at ease when you tell your prospect early on that you'll be taking them back to your office?

_____

_____

_____

_____

_____

D A R E

I dare you today to use the technique above to get each customer back into your office at the end of the sales process. Between customer visits, practice saying the technique aloud to increase your confidence in executing this Dare.

just tell them

reflect

1. Why is it important to tell the buyer that you are going back to the office, versus asking them if they would like to go back? Explain.

_____

_____

_____

_____

_____

_____

2. What happened when you used this Dare today? Explain.

_____

_____

_____

_____

_____

_____

3. What did your customers say when you told them that you would take them back to the sales office?

_____

_____

_____

_____

_____

_____

_____

4. If you consistently execute this Dare with every prospect you see over the next year, how many sales would this strategy earn you? Circle one:

.25 sales   .5 sales   .75 sales   1 sale

1.25 sales   1.5 sales   1.75 sales   2 sales

effort

Rate your effort level towards improving yourself today with this Dare:

1   2   3   4   5   6   7   8   9   10

1: Did not read or do the Dare. 2: Read the Dare, but did not do it. 5: Did the Dare with half of my customers today. 10: Did the Dare with all customers today, and rehearsed the questions between customer encounters.

Dare 24

Create an Experience

read

CUTCO, a company that specializes in high-end knives, doesn't sell its cutlery at Wal-Mart and Target. Instead, associates set up booths where customers can dice tomatoes effortlessly, cleanly trim the excess fat from chicken breasts, and slice through pennies with one squeeze of a pair of scissors. They don't just talk about their knives as tools of superior quality; they create an experience for their prospects. The customer will remember the CUTCO knife the next time they take an inferior blade to a tomato and struggle just to break the skin.

Similarly, creating an experience for your customers allows them to engage with the community amenities rather than just view them from a distance; so take that extra step and carry racquets and balls in your trunk so they can volley back and forth for a bit before they go home. Or take five extra minutes to head out to the playground and chat with your prospects while their kids swing on the monkey bars. Don't limit the experiences to the neighborhood itself. Drive them to the 7-Eleven around the corner and buy a Slurpee, or arrange for tours of the local recreation center. Get creative. This helps your prospects appreciate the amenities, and it emotionally moves them into the community.

Don't just point to an amenity—give your customers an experience they'll want to recreate after they move in.

engage with the community amenities, rather than just look at them from a distance

think

What happens when a customer's experience engages them in a product they are purchasing?

_____

_____

_____

_____

D A R E

I dare you today to give each customer an experience centered on the features in your homes and community. To prepare, write out at least one feature of your home and one feature of your community. Describe how you plan to experience those features with your customers.

reflect

1. What happened when you experientially engaged the customer in your homes and community today?

_____

_____

_____

_____

_____

_____

_____

_____

_____

_____

_____

_____

2. What did you learn about your customers by helping them experience
   your features?

_____

_____

_____

_____

_____

_____

_____

_____

_____

_____

3. By engaging your customers in the community experience, were you
   better equipped to accomplish your customers' goals and, in so doing,
   to improve their lives?

_____

_____

_____

_____

_____

_____

_____

_____

_____

4. If you consistently execute this Dare with every prospect you see over the next year, how many sales would this Dare earn you? Circle one:

.25 sales   .5 sales   .75 sales   1 sale

1.25 sales   1.5 sales   1.75 sales   2 sales

effort

Rate your effort level towards improving yourself today with this Dare:

1   2   3   4   5   6   7   8   9   10

1: Did not read or do the Dare. 2: Read the Dare, but did not do it. 5: Did the Dare with half of my customers today. 10: Did the Dare with all customers today, and rehearsed the questions between customer encounters.

Dare 25

People Can't Argue Emotion, Only Logic

r e a d

My mom is a speech professor and co-author of the public speaking textbook *Shared Meaning*. She says, "When making an argument in a persuasive speech, make points that pull on people's heartstrings. Make your argument around emotion because people can't argue emotion." The principles behind making a persuasive speech relate to the principles of selling.

Your customer can (and likely will) argue if you say, "Buy today because interest rates are going up," or, "This promotion will only last three more days." However, they will have a much harder time arguing with you if you say, "Buy today because you said you needed to be moved in by the start of the school year, and that won't happen unless we get started this week." If you say, "Buy today because you said that your life would be less stressful if your kids had their own rooms," you're just letting your customer chew on the very thing they said was important to them—decreasing stress.

People are more likely to remember a persuasive speaker who tugs on their heartstrings than one who rattles off facts and figures. So, instead of closing your sales presentation with interest rates, close it with images of family game nights and playing with the kids in the backyard. Trust me, people can't argue with emotion.

close with emotion

t h i n k

Track your last ten final arguments. Did you make your final arguments around emotion, or around logic? If you are leaning more towards logic, determine why you are discounting emotions.

_____

_____

_____

_____

D A R E

I dare you today to make your final arguments to your customers based upon emotion and not logic. Practice between customer visits to increase your comfort and confidence with this new technique.

r e f l e c t

1. Were you comfortable or uncomfortable in using this technique today? If you were uncomfortable, was it because you are not used to doing it, because you disagree with the concept, or for another reason? If you disagree, consider why.

_____

_____

_____

_____

_____

_____

2. Write out an example of how you used today's Dare:

_____

_____

_____

_____

_____

In the example you wrote above, consider the results and describe what happened, as well as what the customer said, when you used today's Dare.

_____

_____

_____

_____

_____

_____

3. If you consistently execute this Dare with every prospect you see over the next year, how many sales would this Dare earn you? Circle one:

   .25 sales   .5 sales   .75 sales   1 sale

   1.25 sales   1.5 sales   1.75 sales   2 sales

effort

Rate your effort level towards improving yourself today with this Dare:

1   2   3   4   5   6   7   8   9   10

1: Did not read or do the Dare. 2: Read the Dare, but did not do it. 5: Did the Dare with half of my customers today. 10: Did the Dare with all customers today, and rehearsed the questions between customer encounters.

Dare 26

Three Simple Phrases

read

I was watching a secret video shop of a salesperson who said three phrases that made certain she accomplished the customer's mission. The sentences started with:

- "You mentioned…"
- "How would this space work… ?"
- and "Why?"

In her case, it went like this: "You mentioned you needed a space for your grand piano—how would this space work for you, and why does this space work for you?" These phrases are so simple, yet so powerful.

First, she showed that she was actively listening by bringing the piano back up after the customer had mentioned it. Second, she held him accountable to making a decision that accomplished one of his particular goals. Third, she got the customer involved emotionally in the decision by having him tell her why it would work. Remember, selling is all about decisions. The customer comes in with a list of expectations that must be met for them to feel good about buying a home. It is your job to take ownership of those customer decisions. When you help the customer make decisions faster than they would by themselves, you increase the probability that they'll choose to buy their next home from you.

take ownership - help them make decisions

think

How do you view your role in the customer's decision-making process? Do you perceive yourself as a leader who works to speed up the process? Or, do you see yourself as someone who is there only when the customer has questions or concerns?

_____

_____

_____

_____

DARE

I dare you today to actively listen to your customers so that you can understand all of the decisions they need to make before purchasing from you. Then, use these simple yet powerful phrases:

- "You mentioned…"
- "How would this _(space, kitchen, backyard, etc.)_ work for you?"
- and "Why does it work for you (or not work for you)?"

Do this with every customer you speak to today, and practice the technique between customer visits.

reflect

1. What happened when you actively listened to your customers today? How did it prepare you for the sales presentation?

_____

_____

_____

_____

_____

_____

_____

_____

2. What happened when you used the three phrases, "You mentioned...", "How does this _____ work?" and "Why does it work/not work for you?"

_____

_____

_____

_____

_____

_____

_____

_____

3. By using those three phrases, how were you able to take the leadership role in the decision-making process?

_____

_____

_____

_____

_____

_____

_____

_____

_____

4. If you consistently execute this Dare with every prospect you see over the next year, how many sales would this Dare earn you? Circle one:

Week 4 | Dare 26

    .25 sales   .5 sales   .75 sales   1 sale

    1.25 sales   1.5 sales   1.75 sales   2 sales

effort

Rate your effort level towards improving yourself today with this Dare:

1   2   3   4   5   6   7   8   9   10

1: Did not read or do the Dare. 2: Read the Dare, but did not do it. 5: Did the Dare with half of my customers today. 10: Did the Dare with all customers today, and rehearsed the questions between customer encounters.

Week 4
Day-Off Dares

"You cannot wait for buyers
to walk in the door with their
checkbooks out. You must create
a sense of urgency for them."

Dare 27
Don't Wait For Urgency — Create It

read

My wife and I were Christmas shopping when a salesperson approached and asked, "Can I show you something amazing?" I wasn't interested, but my wife said yes, so we went along. The salesperson asked me and Shelly to open our hands palm up, and then she dropped a dollop of sea salt scrub onto them. While we were rubbing the scrub over our hands, she asked what we did for a living. I was in new home sales, so she wanted to know how often I shook people's hands. We continued the discussion as she poured a pitcher of water over our hands. After we'd washed off the scrub, she threw a towel over my hands, patted them dry and asked, "So how do they feel?" They felt good, as it turned out—very smooth. She turned to Shelly and asked, "Do you think the people who shake hands with your husband every day would be impressed if his hands felt like this?" I looked at Shelly, and then back at the salesperson. "We'll take two."

This salesperson created an experience that made me think about what my hands felt like to customers. So even though I wasn't going to the mall for sea salt scrub, I left with two jars: one for the office and one for home.

As salespeople, you cannot wait for buyers to walk in the door with their checkbooks out. You must create a sense of urgency for them. Just like my sea salt scrub salesperson, you must learn to turn a "no" into a "yes."

159

think

Are you a salesperson who believes that customers will come to see you with urgency; or do you believe that it is your sole purpose to create urgency within your customers?

_____

_____

_____

_____

D A R E

I dare you to go to your nearby mall today and study salespeople. Take note of the people who create urgency, and compare them to the ones who wait for customers to come to them. What's different in the manner of these salespeople? How do they successfully create urgency? What are they doing that the other salespeople are not doing?

reflect

1. What are the traits of the salespeople who created urgency?

_____

_____

_____

_____

_____

_____

_____

2. What are the traits of the salespeople who waited for people to come in with urgency?

_____

_____

_____

_____

_____

_____

_____

3. What did you learn about your own sales presentation?

_____

_____

_____

_____

_____

_____

_____

4. What do you plan on doing differently, starting this week?

_____

_____

_____

_____

_____

_____

_____

_____

5. If you consistently take ownership over creating urgency with every
    prospect you see over the next year, how many sales would this Dare
    earn you?

    .25 sales   .5 sales   .75 sales   1 sale

    1.25 sales   1.5 sales   1.75 sales   2 sales

e f f o r t

Rate your effort level towards improving yourself today with this Dare:

1   2   3   4   5   6   7   8   9   10

1: Did not read or do the Dare. 2: Read the Dare, but did not do it. 5: Did the Dare with half of my customers today. 10: Did the Dare with all customers today, and rehearsed the questions between customer encounters.

Dare 28

Spend the Time

r e a d

You've heard the saying: "It's quality that matters, not quantity." A salesperson I know from Phoenix decided to test the theory in relation to how much time he spent with his prospects. He told his sales partner that she could have all of the new customers that came in while he was with his existing clients. Further, in a community with more than forty new visitors per week, he wanted only ten. His goal was to take those ten as far in the sales process as he could, and spend the rest of his time nurturing and following up with the buyers already in his pipeline.

His strategy was to slow down and focus on one buyer at time. He didn't jeopardize the relationship by trying to qualify them too early; he just focused on understanding the customer's mission to improve their life. He worked *for* his prospects, dutifully searching out the best home and solving their mission. He didn't worry about the customers he might be missing. He focused on performing perfectly with each buyer and kept a journal of how he did, what mistakes he made, and what he could learn from those mistakes. In addition to improving his performance with each individual customer, he also found that he got more satisfaction out of getting to know his buyers and solving their problems.

I know, I know. What you really want to know is if the gamble worked. Well, in two months he was averaging four sales per month, and his partner was averaging two. She had *four times* as much traffic, but he had *twice as many sales.* In the end, our little gambler had doubled his yearly income! Yeah, I'd say it worked, and that's why I'll sing the praises of "quality, not quantity" to all who will listen.

t h i n k

What is your biggest fear about focusing on one customer and taking them as far as you can in the sales process? Do you think it's possible that by slowing down and focusing on quality, you might sell more?

_____

_____

_____

_____

D A R E

I dare you this week to focus on just one customer at a time, taking them as far as you can in the sales process. Do not worry about who you might be missing, but instead focus on what you are accomplishing with that one buyer.

r e f l e c t

1. Which of the following scenarios do you believe will give you a higher probability of selling more? Circle one:
    *   90 minutes per customer with 10 customers per week
    *   30 minutes per customer with 30 customers per week

2. What happened today when you focused on taking just one customer at a time as far as you could in the sales process? Did you find yourself less distracted and more equipped to focus on performing perfectly with that one customer?

_____

_____

_____

_____

_____

_____

_____

3. If you consistently execute this Dare with every prospect you see over the next year, how many sales would this Dare earn you? Circle one:

.25 sales   .5 sales   .75 sales   1 sale

1.25 sales   1.5 sales   1.75 sales   2 sales

effort

Rate your effort level towards improving yourself today with this Dare:

1   2   3   4   5   6   7   8   9   10

1: Did not read or do the Dare. 2: Read the Dare, but did not do it. 5: Did the Dare with half of my customers today. 10: Did the Dare with all customers today, and rehearsed the questions between customer encounters.

Slow down and focus on one buyer at a time.

Week 4 Summary

Before you continue in your journey towards improvement, take a moment to get your bearings by completing your Week 4 Summary. **You must do this before you continue to Week 5.**

Average Effort Score for Week 4:

Review your Effort Scores from Dares 22-28, and calculate your Average Effort Score for the week. Write it in the space below.

_____

4 or less = It's time to get serious. Recommit yourself to the program, and start fresh in Week 5 by striving for a 5 or higher each day!

5 to 7 = You're doing well, but you can do even better! Make a commitment today to raise the bar for yourself in Week 5, and strive for an average of 8 or better.

8 to 9 = What a great week! Keep pushing forward, and make it your personal goal to score all 9's and 10's in Week 5.

10 = Excellent! You are a rock star. If you maintain this effort level, you will receive the maximum benefit from this program, and you will achieve the success that you desire.

What's it worth?

What was this week worth to you? Flip back through Week 4, and tally the number of sales that you said Dares 22-28 would earn you. Write it below.

_____

28 Dares down... just 12 to go!
You can do it!

Week 5

Dares 29-35

Day-On Dares

_____ 29. What If They Say No?

_____ 30. Be the Connector

_____ 31. Create the Wish List

_____ 32. People Can't Argue with Their Own Advice

_____ 33. Start at the Very Beginning

Day-Off Dares

_____ 34. Pressure vs Stress

_____ 35. From Breaking Dirt to Hitting Pay Dirt

"You're just helping them make a decision that gets them one step closer to their goal."

Dare 29

What If They Say No?

read

This year, I conducted a study of 100 salespeople. I looked for unsuccessful habits, trends in behavior, and traits that led to success. Out of the 100 salespeople I observed, **only one** salesperson asked his customers for the sale twice during their visit.

Think about your own experiences. When have you ever purchased anything from a salesperson the first time they asked? If you are like most people, your reflexive response to the salesperson is, "No," but inside, the wheels start turning and you're considering whether you should or should not move forward with the purchase. That's when the real questions and concerns come up. If the salesperson would only continue the conversation and ask questions to uncover those concerns, you would probably realize that there is nothing to fear, and you might even end up purchasing the item you initially declined. This is also true of the customers you see every day.

You must look at asking for the sale as helping your customers achieve a resolution to their quest. They told you that your home would improve their lives, so you're just helping them make a decision that gets them one step closer to *their* goal. When they say no to your first closing attempt, use that as a springboard to find out what's not quite right. You can say,

"If we have found the home that you said would be perfect for you and your family, then what are your concerns? Is there something that you are not happy with, or are you just uncomfortable making such a huge decision?"

If they admit their discomfort, then say,

"I understand your fear. Buying a home is a big deal, but I feel confident that we've been thorough in accomplishing everything that you said you desired in your next home. Do you feel that we have missed anything?"

If you have missed something, or if they bring up a hidden desire, then address it. On the other hand, if they agree that this is the best home, then say, "I will be here for you every step of the way and would be honored to have you as the newest resident in River Park. What do you think?"

Even if they say no to your second attempt, they know that you really desire to have them in your community. That's a great thing, and it will grant you a higher status in their minds than any other salesperson they meet. If they say yes, and many of them will, you have accomplished another sale.

think

If a customer believes your home is the best home for them, do you feel that asking them to purchase twice in the same visit will hurt your chances of making a sale, or take you one step closer? Why?

_____

_____

_____

_____

look at asking for the sale as helping my customers achieve a resolution

DARE

I dare you today to ask every customer twice for the sale. Memorize and use the script above when a customer says no to your first closing attempt.

reflect

1. How did this Dare change your perception about asking for the sale twice during the same visit? Explain.

_____

_____

_____

_____

_____

_____

_____

2. What happened when you used this Dare today? What did you learn about the customer and yourself?

_____

_____

_____

_____

_____

_____

_____

_____

3. If you consistently execute this Dare with every prospect you see over
    the next year, how many sales would this strategy earn you? Circle one:

    .25 sales   .5 sales   .75 sales   1 sale

    1.25 sales   1.5 sales   1.75 sales   2 sales

e f f o r t

Rate your effort level towards improving yourself today with this Dare:

1   2   3   4   5   6   7   8   9   10

1: Did not read or do the Dare. 2: Read the Dare, but did not do it. 5: Did the Dare with half of my customers today. 10: Did the Dare with all customers today, and rehearsed the questions between customer encounters.

Dare 30

Be the Connector

r e a d

George Gallup has said, "Americans are among the loneliest people in the world." Think about it. We drive straight into our garages and only venture out to our fenced backyards to play with the kids or to barbecue.

Though as a society we have strayed far from the practice of interacting regularly with neighbors, we are still humans, and humans long for community. If you can give your prospects the sense that they'll fit in when they go down the street to the playground, they'll be that much more likely to buy your home rather than the one offered in the next neighborhood. So get to know the chatty neighbors, and stop and talk to people while they're out mowing their lawn. That way, when you're driving a prospect to Lot 17, you can stop and introduce them to their "new neighbors."

If they're deciding between two comparable communities, your prospects are more likely to choose the one where they already feel like they'll fit. By introducing them around, you'll give them a head start. Salespeople are usually connectors by nature, so do what you do best—connect your prospects to their future neighbors.

We long for community.
People are more likely to choose the
community where they feel like they'll fit.

think

How would it benefit your customers if you connected them to others in the community? How much sooner will they build friendships if you are the catalyst?

_____

_____

_____

_____

DARE

I dare you today to make a list of residents who would be good at welcoming future homeowners, and contact those residents. Then make a list of current residents who are home during the day, and contact them to see if they would be receptive to meeting potential homeowners.

reflect

1. Did you call your current residents today? Circle one: YES NO
   Note: If the answer is Yes, then congratulate yourself for investing in your career and move on to Question 2. If the answer is No, consider why you didn't make the calls to your customers:

   a. Was it uncomfortable?

   b. Were you afraid of what they would say?

   c. Did you forget?

2. What did you learn about your residents from calling them?

_____

_____

_____

_____

_____

_____

3. Did you stop today to introduce your customer to a current resident? How do you think that affected your sales presentation?

_____

_____

_____

_____

_____

_____

_____

_____

4. By being the connector, are you better equipped to accomplish your customers' goals and, in so doing, to improve their lives? Explain.

_____

_____

_____

_____

_____

_____

_____

_____

5. If you consistently execute this Dare with every prospect you see over the next year, how many sales would this Dare earn you? Circle one:

.25 sales   .5 sales   .75 sales   1 sale

1.25 sales   1.5 sales   1.75 sales   2 sales

e f f o r t

Rate your effort level towards improving yourself today with this Dare:

1   2   3   4   5   6   7   8   9   10

1: Did not read or do the Dare. 2: Read the Dare, but did not do it. 5: Did the Dare with half of my customers today. 10: Did the Dare with all customers today, and rehearsed the questions between customer encounters.

Dare 31

read

When ballroom dancers are in sync, one partner leads and the other follows. There is an emotional connection that goes beyond memorizing the steps. The result is a fluid movement that appears effortless. It's magic.

The magic is lost, though, when partners lose their connection, and thus, the rhythm of the dance. They focus too much on the nuts and bolts of the technique, and they start looking at their feet instead of their partner's eyes.

Showing a home can be a lot like a dance. When you're in your groove, it's fun for you and for your customer. You follow each other's cues. It's natural and unforced. On the other hand, when it feels forced or even manipulated, demonstrating the home can be uncomfortable and tense.

One of the easiest ways to lose your selling rhythm is to get bogged down in the "standard versus optional" discussion. This is like looking down at your feet during a dance. You lose the emotional connection with the buyer, and thus the opportunity to engage them in the home on a personal level.

Here's a hint: as the Salesperson, you're the Leader. Think about it. You know your community and homes better than anyone else, so take a proactive approach. Before walking into the first home, say:

177

"In each of our models, we showcase both the included features and the optional features so that you can see our flexibility in tailoring the home to meet your unique taste. While we go through the home, if you are interested in a particular feature you see, let me know and I will put it on your wish list. Then at the end of our walk, I will go back and create a master list of all the options that caught your eye, along with their prices."

This lets you maintain the emotional connection with your customer. Dancing is more fun for everyone when you're not looking at your feet.

t h i n k

The selling rhythm allows you to remain in control of the experience. It also gives you a specific reason to sit down with your client at the end of the presentation and review their wish list. List two of your own reasons for why the selling rhythm is so important.

_____

_____

_____

_____

D A R E

I dare you today to proactively tell each customer about creating a wish list. Don't worry about creating your own version of the script, but instead just memorize the one given to you above. Once you get comfortable using the script, then you can make it your own.

reflect

1. How did using the script feel?

_____

_____

_____

_____

_____

_____

_____

_____

2. With what percentage of your customers did you use the script?

    _____%

    Note: If the answer is 100%, then congratulate yourself for investing in your career and move on to Question 3. For anything less than 100 %, consider why you didn't ask each question to each customer:

    a. Was it uncomfortable?

    b. Were you afraid of what the customer would say?

    c. Did you forget?

3. Were you able to stay in control of the customer presentation versus becoming stuck in the "standard versus optional" tour? Explain.

_____

_____

_____

_____

_____

_____

_____

_____

4. Did you use the wish list as a reason to sit back down with the customer at the very end of the presentation? Explain.

_____

_____

_____

_____

_____

_____

_____

5. If you consistently execute this Dare with every prospect you see over the next year, how many sales would this Dare earn you? Circle one:

.25 sales   .5 sales   .75 sales   1 sale

1.25 sales   1.5 sales   1.75 sales   2 sales

effort

Rate your effort level towards improving yourself today with this Dare:

1   2   3   4   5   6   7   8   9   10

1: Did not read or do the Dare. 2: Read the Dare, but did not do it. 5: Did the Dare with half of my customers today. 10: Did the Dare with all customers today, and rehearsed the questions between customer encounters.

One of the easiest ways to lose my selling rhythm is to get bogged down in the "standard versus optional" discussion.

Let your customer tell you
their own solution.

Dare 32

People Can't Argue
with Their Own Advice

r e a d

"You tell me" is one of the most powerful phrases that you can use to handle customer concerns. I recently watched a salesperson use this strategy successfully for three objections in a row. In one, the customer felt the kitchen was too dark. The salesperson said, "OK, well, you tell me how you would fix it." The customer described how the lighting in the adjacent room would help and how she could add under-cabinet lights and a lamp. It was amazing. Without providing a solution and with only three words, the salesperson solved the objection.

When you say to a customer, "You tell me," one of two things will happen: either 1) your customer will come up with their own solution, or 2) you'll buy yourself some time to come up with an adequate answer. Either way, you are better off holding your tongue and saying, "You tell me."

t h i n k

Do you feel that you always have to be the one to come up with the solution? If so, why? In the last week, for which objections could your customers have created their own solutions?

_____

_____

_____

_____

D A R E

I dare you today to say, "You tell me what you would do," when your customers have objections.

r e f l e c t

1. Write out a specific example of an objection that you used this technique on today.

_____

_____

_____

_____

_____

_____

_____

2. What happened?

_____

_____

_____

_____

_____

_____

_____

3. How will using "you tell me" benefit you with future objections?

_____

_____

_____

_____

_____

4. If you consistently execute this Dare with every prospect you see over the next year, how many sales would this Dare earn you? Circle one:

.25 sales   .5 sales   .75 sales   1 sale

1.25 sales   1.5 sales   1.75 sales   2 sales

effort

Rate your effort level towards improving yourself today with this Dare:

1   2   3   4   5   6   7   8   9   10

1: Did not read or do the Dare. 2: Read the Dare, but did not do it. 5: Did the Dare with half of my customers today. 10: Did the Dare with all customers today, and rehearsed the questions between customer encounters.

"Your customers will appreciate that you took the time to explain what's unique about the community they're considering calling home."

Dare 33

Start at the Very Beginning

read

"I'm not kidnapping you, but I have a purpose here." As a new home salesperson, I often started my tours with such a statement, and then drove my prospects to the community entrance. I'd stop the car and explain that they were looking at what their friends and family would first see when they came to visit. I'd point out the material of the entrance sign, the vibrant colors of the landscaping and any other unique aspects of the entrance.

Remember, developers don't just buy a piece of land and start building. Like floor plans, which go through rigorous testing before they ever see the light of day, communities only become communities after developers carefully plan each detail. They consider the area's terrain, its place in the neighboring environment, and the way the streetscape will look in years to come. So after I showed my customers the entrance, I'd continue driving, pointing out the special touches the builder put into the streetscape, the sidewalks and the community layout.

Your customers will appreciate that you took the time to explain what's unique about the community they're considering calling home. So take Julie Andrews' advice and start at the very beginning; it's the very best place to start.

t h i n k

Ask sales managers and developers why the homes are spaced the way they are, and how they planned the street layout. Write the answers down. Now, rewrite them into statements such as "When the developers envisioned this community, they had _____ in mind."

_____

_____

_____

_____

_____

_____

_____

_____

_____

_____

D A R E

I dare you today to discover the reasoning behind your community's layout and features. I dare you to share these statements with every client you show a home to today.

remember: developers don't just buy a piece of land and start building

reflect

1. How would the community developer explain to your customers his/ her vision for the completed project? How does that compare to your explanation? Do you sound like you have the same passion for the community as the developer does? Do you own the words you're saying, as if you were talking about your own creation or vision?

_____

_____

_____

_____

_____

_____

_____

2. What did you learn about your community that you did not know?

_____

_____

_____

_____

_____

_____

3. What happened when you took the customer to the front of the neighborhood and shared the vision of the community from their future visitors' point of view?

_____

_____

_____

_____

_____

_____

4. How did starting at the entrance enhance the customer experience?

_____

_____

_____

_____

_____

_____

_____

_____

5. If you consistently execute this Dare with every prospect you see over the next year, how many sales would this Dare earn you? Circle one:

.25 sales   .5 sales   .75 sales   1 sale

1.25 sales   1.5 sales   1.75 sales   2 sales

effort

Rate your effort level towards improving yourself today with this Dare:

1   2   3   4   5   6   7   8   9   10

1: Did not read or do the Dare. 2: Read the Dare, but did not do it. 5: Did the Dare with half of my customers today. 10: Did the Dare with all customers today, and rehearsed the questions between customer encounters.

Week 5
Day-Off Dares

"... when we've done everything in our power to succeed, we might feel pressure, but not stress."

Dare 34

Pressure vs Stress

read

As an alumni advisor for my fraternity, I hear about final exam week every year. Inevitably, I remember my own college days and how I handled (and sometimes did not handle) final exam week. Sometimes I spent the month before exams hanging out with my friends and watching TV. Then on the night before the exam, I drank gallons of coffee and crammed. I'd approach the test exhausted, uncertain and stressed beyond belief because I had not prepared. Other times though, I'd spend the month before the exam in the library or at my desk—books open and mind focused. I'd review my notes on the night before and then go to bed early. I'd wake up prepared and confident. Would I feel some pressure to do a great job? Sure I would, but I would not feel stress. I would take the test with confidence because I knew I had prepared.

The problem for many of us is that when we have "final exams," such as making our sales numbers, we feel stressed and uncertain. The difference, though, is when we've done everything in our power to succeed, we might feel pressure, but not stress.

Remember, in work as in life, we are measured not by our failures, but by our ability to look our failures in the eye and come back faster, stronger, and better.

What objections are you struggling with that you must learn to overcome? Which stages of the sales process are these objections bringing to a halt? What can you do, or learn to do, in order to keep the sale moving forward at that stage?

At the end of each day, ask yourself if you accomplished all your action points for that day.

t h i n k

Do you feel pressure or stress to make your sales goals this month? If you feel stress, write down three things you can do to be better prepared.

_____

_____

_____

_____

D A R E

I dare you today to write out daily goals for the next week. At the beginning of each day, remind yourself of what you must accomplish on that day to get closer to reaching your income goal.

r e f l e c t

1. Write down your success strategy to achieve your sales goals during the next thirty days. The success strategy should include what you believe

are the everyday behaviors that you should do to give you the highest probability of reaching your income goal.

_____

_____

_____

_____

_____

_____

_____

_____

2. If you consistently execute this Dare every day over the next year, how many sales would this Dare earn you? Circle one:

.25 sales   .5 sales   .75 sales   1 sale

1.25 sales   1.5 sales   1.75 sales   2 sales

effort

Rate your effort level towards improving yourself today with this Dare:

1   2   3   4   5   6   7   8   9   10

1: Did not read or do the Dare. 2: Read the Dare, but did not do it. 5: Did the Dare with half of my customers today. 10: Did the Dare with all customers today, and rehearsed the questions between customer encounters.

Daily Incentives provide:
1) instant gratification
2) opportunity for accountability

day off

Dare 35

From Breaking Dirt
to Hitting Pay Dirt

r e a d

I started my new home sales career in a community with a nine-month build cycle and no inventory. No inventory means no quick money, and a nine-month build cycle means a long wait for that first check. I was excited to eventually break even on my draw and then to exceed it, but I needed daily motivation for the big money in the distance. And I needed someone to hold me accountable.

For me, that someone was my wife. Shelly and I agreed that every time I took a contract to start building a home, I could buy a custom-made shirt. This gave me daily incentive by providing instant gratification, and it allowed her to hold me accountable. Every night she'd ask, "Were you able to buy a new shirt tonight?" The $75 I spent on each shirt was no big deal—it was just a short-term investment towards the $3,000 payoff ahead. I was younger then, so my priorities were different, but the principle remains. The "instant gratification" strategy kept me focused on what I needed to do to be successful.

t h i n k

Are you going at this alone? Who is one person you can call today to help keep you accountable for your success?

Week 5 | Dare 35

199

DARE

I dare you today to ask at least one person to be part of your support group. Tell them what you are doing and how they can help you by holding you accountable. Come up with an immediate gratification reward.

reflect

1. Who can be in your support group?

_____

_____

_____

_____

_____

2. Write out what you are going to ask them to do in order to keep you accountable.

_____

_____

_____

_____

_____

3. How often would you like them to contact you to ask the accountability question?

_____

_____

4. Write down an immediate gratification reward—something you can buy yourself or do for yourself every time you sell a home.

_____

_____

_____

_____

5. If you consistently focused on an immediate gratification reward, and had a support person hold you accountable, how many sales would this Dare earn you over the next year? Circle one:

```
.25 sales    .5 sales    .75 sales    1 sale
1.25 sales   1.5 sales   1.75 sales   2 sales
```

e f f o r t

Rate your effort level towards improving yourself today with this Dare:

```
1   2   3   4   5   6   7   8   9   10
```

1: Did not read or do the Dare. 2: Read the Dare, but did not do it. 5: Did the Dare with half of my customers today. 10: Did the Dare with all customers today, and rehearsed the questions between customer encounters.

Week 5 Summary

Before you continue in your journey towards improvement, take a moment to get your bearings by completing your Week 5 Summary. **You must do this before you continue to Week 6.**

Average Effort Score for Week 5:

Review your Effort Scores from Dares 29-35, and calculate your Average Effort Score for the week. Write it in the space below.

_____

4 or less = It's time to get serious. Recommit yourself to the program, and start fresh in Week 6 by striving for a 5 or higher each day!

5 to 7 = You're doing well, but you can do even better! Make a commitment today to raise the bar for yourself in Week 6, and strive for an average of 8 or better.

8 to 9 = What a great week! Keep pushing forward, and make it your personal goal to score all 9's and 10's in Week 6.

10 = Excellent! You are a rock star. If you maintain this effort level, you will receive the maximum benefit from this program, and you will achieve the success that you desire.

What's it worth?

What was this week worth to you? Flip back through Week 5, and tally the number of sales that you said Dares 29-35 would earn you. Write it below.

_____

35 Dares down... only 5 to go!
You can do it!

Week 6

Dares 36-40

Day-On Dares

_____ 36. Selling the Intangible

_____ 37. One-Hour Follow-Up

_____ 38. Give Them an Assignment

Day-Off Dares

_____ 39. Effort or Ability?

_____ 40. Stump Me Twice, Shame on Me

"You must sell what your
customers are looking for:
their very own 'third place.'"

Dare 36

Selling the Intangible

r e a d

Starbucks made the concept of the "third place" famous, but the idea isn't new. In the sitcom *Cheers*, Norm Peterson's "third place" is the namesake bar where everybody knows your name. It's that place of comfort, social interaction, and community that is neither the home nor the office.

When you are selling tangible amenities like parks, walking paths, and golf courses, you must sell what your customers are really looking for: their very own "third place." This "third place" is not just the playground, but also the conversations the stay-at-home mom will have on the playground, and the books she'll read on the bench while her kids are playing. For the active young professional, sell the time to unwind and exercise after a stressful day rather than the walking path itself. Don't sell the golf course to that busy dad; sell the time he'll have with his buddies to talk about everything *but* golf. Don't just sell your prospects on a community; sell them on the sense of community they'll find on that park bench, or while playing golf with their neighbors.

t h i n k

In the following table, there are two columns and three rows. In the left column, you will write down at least three amenities that you have in your community or homes. In the right column, for each of those amenities, write at least one statement or question that you can use to get the customer thinking about the intangible aspects of the feature.

Amenities (at least 3)	Statements / Questions
1.	
2.	
3.	

DARE

I dare you today to use at least one of your amenities with every customer you talk to. While you are demonstrating your amenity, use your intangible statements or questions to get the customer thinking emotionally.

reflect

1. How did using these questions or statements feel?

_____

_____

_____

_____

_____

2. With what percentage of your customers did you ask a question or use a statement?

_____%

Note: If the answer is 100%, then congratulate yourself for investing in your career and move on to Question 3. For anything less than 100%, consider why you didn't ask each question to each customer:

a. Was it uncomfortable?

b. Were you afraid of the answer?

c. Did you forget?

3. What did you learn about your customers from using these statements and questions?

_____

_____

_____

_____

_____

_____

_____

4. By asking these questions, were you better equipped to accomplish your customers' goals and, in so doing, to improve their lives?

_____

_____

_____

_____

_____

5. If you consistently execute this Dare with every prospect you see over the next year, how many sales would this Dare earn you? Circle one:

.25 sales   .5 sales   .75 sales   1 sale

1.25 sales   1.5 sales   1.75 sales   2 sales

e f f o r t

Rate your effort level towards improving yourself today with this Dare:

1   2   3   4   5   6   7   8   9   10

1: Did not read or do the Dare. 2: Read the Dare, but did not do it. 5: Did the Dare with half of my customers today. 10: Did the Dare with all customers today, and rehearsed the questions between customer encounters.

"Your biggest competitor is
the conversation your customer
will have about you and your
community once they leave."

Dare 37

One-Hour Follow-Up

r e a d

Who or what is your biggest competitor? Is it the market, the economy, or maybe the competing neighborhoods and builders? While all of these factors play into your buyer's decision, the answer isn't in the list above. Your biggest competitor is the conversation your customer will have about you and your community once they leave.

On their way out the door (and down the street or around the block to another builder), your customers are talking about you and thinking of several questions and concerns about your community. They're asking their significant other, "What about this?" and, "What if that?" Chances are, they're not going to call you to find out the answers. They're just going to keep moving forward—right into one of your competitor's homes.

How do you combat this? *You* call them while all those questions and concerns are still fresh. This gives you the best opportunity to address all their questions and put their minds at ease. It also helps you establish your credibility as a professional who cares about his/her prospects.

So don't wait until next week when you "have a minute" to make those follow-up calls. *Create* the time today and get ready to create yourself a contract.

t h i n k

Write down a past experience when you were shopping for something, did not make a decision, had a question, but left without asking the salesperson. Don't you wish you would have asked your question while you were there? Now, what would have happened if the salesperson had called you and said,

> "Thanks for spending time with me today. Whenever I leave a store, I usually have a question that I wished I would have asked but forgot to. Did that happen to you? Do you have any additional questions that I could answer for you?"

_____

_____

_____

_____

D A R E

I dare you today to call every one of your prospects within one hour after they walk out your door.

r e f l e c t

1. What happened when you called your prospects today?

_____

_____

_____

_____

_____

_____

_____

_____

_____

_____

2. Write down one example of someone you called and the resulting con-
    versation.

_____

_____

_____

_____

_____

_____

_____

3. Did it help or hurt your probability of moving the sale forward? Why?

_____

_____

_____

_____

_____

_____

_____

_____

4. How do you feel your customers perceived you on the phone?

    a. "This salesperson really wants to help and make this process as easy as possible for us?"

    b. Or, "This salesperson is so pushy."

Which perception did you choose, and why?

_____

_____

_____

_____

_____

_____

_____

_____

_____

_____

5. In the end, was calling your prospects within one hour worth doing? Why?

_____

_____

_____

_____

_____

_____

_____

6. If you consistently execute this Dare with every prospect you see over the next year, how many sales would this Dare earn you? Circle one:

.25 sales   .5 sales   .75 sales   1 sale

1.25 sales   1.5 sales   1.75 sales   2 sales

effort

Rate your effort level towards improving yourself today with this Dare:

1   2   3   4   5   6   7   8   9   10

1: Did not read or do the Dare. 2: Read the Dare, but did not do it. 5: Did the Dare with half of my customers today. 10: Did the Dare with all customers today, and rehearsed the questions between customer encounters.

You want your customers to compare the other builders to your standard, not the other way around.

Dare 38

Give Them an Assignment

read

What do you do when your customers love your homes and community, but simply won't commit? Well, you can demonstrate confidence in your brand and help push them toward a decision with one simple act. Send them on their way with a personalized "dare to compare" sheet.

This is how it works. You get out a piece of paper and a red marker and say,

> "I understand that you want to look around. Since I have a strong sense of what you're looking for, I'd like to help make your search as easy as possible. Let's summarize what you need in your next home."

While you restate what they've told you, write the items down. As you list their needs, focus on the areas that make your community different from your competition so that your customers will compare the other builders to *your* standard, not the other way around. When you're done say,

> "This should make your house-hunting adventure easier, don't you think? More than anything, I hope you find the best home for you and your family. Good luck!"

If you don't see them within 24 hours, call and ask how the sheet is working for them. Ideally, they'll return to you with the paper in hand—red markings all over it. In this case, welcome them back and ask them how the

217

list helped them in finding their next home. Simply by returning, they're giving a strong signal that they want what you have to offer. So give it to them.

think

What does it say about your confidence in your product when you give your clients a personalized "dare to compare" sheet?

_____

_____

_____

_____

DARE

I dare you today to give every customer the personalized "dare to compare" sheet before they walk out your door. (This is not a standardized marketing sheet that every customer receives.)

reflect

1. How did it feel to be able to create a personalized "dare to compare" sheet with your customers today? Did it give you a sense of accomplishment that you were able to take the customer as far as possible today?

_____

_____

_____

_____

_____

_____

_____

_____

_____

2. How will this technique help you in following up with your customers?

_____

_____

_____

_____

_____

_____

_____

_____

3. How will creating a personalized "dare to compare" sheet give you a competitive advantage? What does it say about you in the minds of your customers?

_____

_____

_____

If I don't hear from them within 24 hours, I need to call and ask how the sheet is working for them.

_____

_____

_____

_____

_____

_____

4. If you consistently execute this Dare with every prospect you see over
    the next year, how many sales would this Dare earn you? Circle one:

    .25 sales   .5 sales   .75 sales   1 sale

    1.25 sales   1.5 sales   1.75 sales   2 sales

e f f o r t

Rate your effort level towards improving yourself today with this Dare:

1   2   3   4   5   6   7   8   9   10

1: Did not read or do the Dare. 2: Read the Dare, but did not do it. 5: Did the Dare with half of my customers today. 10: Did the Dare with all customers today, and rehearsed the questions between customer encounters.

Week 6
Day-Off Dares

"What sets an average
salesperson apart from an
exceptional one?"

Dare 39

Effort or Ability?

read

"If a man is called to be a street sweeper, he would sweep streets even as Michelangelo painted, or Beethoven composed music, or Shakespeare wrote poetry. He should sweep streets so well that all the hosts of heaven and earth will pause to say, 'Here lived a great street sweeper who did his job well.'" — Dr. Martin Luther King, Jr.

Congratulations, you're a salesperson. You wrote a resume that caught someone's eye, you demonstrated your professionalism in the interviews, and you passed the tests. The social skills that come naturally to you border upon painful to someone else. If you've made it this far, you have "the stuff." So what sets an average salesperson apart from an exceptional one?

Dr. King's examples were prolific artists in their respective fields; but it's easy to take for granted the time they spent chiseling, composing, or writing and rewriting with quill in hand. You had better believe that as they fell asleep at night, Michelangelo visualized his next subject, Beethoven composed new melodies, and Shakespeare spun new plots.

The truth is, we never would have heard of Michelangelo if he hadn't expended an enormous amount of effort. He sculpted at least 42 major works in addition to his large body of paintings. Beethoven composed hundreds of pieces ranging from solos to full symphonies, and Shakespeare wrote more than 40 plays and enough poetry to fill volumes.

223

Often we look at the success of those at the top of their fields, and dismiss it as unattainable. We use "they're special" or "I'll never be that good" as excuses to not spend the energy and time necessary to excel. How many more Michelangelos, Beethovens and Shakespeares would we have if everyone put that much effort into their gifts?

t h i n k

How much more money would you have in the bank if you put that kind of effort into your trade?

_____

_____

_____

_____

D A R E

I dare you to put forth the level of effort that Dr. King speaks of, and to do that every day from this day forward. See what happens to your success.

r e f l e c t

1. In the table below, there are two columns. In the left column, write down three activities/skills that you are good at (photography, video games, basketball, etc.). In the right column, write down how much time you spend thinking about or doing those activities on an average day.

Activities/Skills that I'm good at	Time Spent
1.	
2.	
3.	

2. Now, in the left column below, write down three activities/skills that you admire in others but aren't so good at (public speaking, writing, math, study skills, etc.) and in the right column, write how much time you spend thinking about or doing these activities on an average day.

Activities/Skills that I'm not good at	Time Spent
1.	
2.	
3.	

3. What's the difference between the first group and the second group?

_____

_____

If you're like me, you spend more time on the first three activities. So, how can you become better at the items in the second group? What's the solution? Spend just as much time in the areas that you are not as good at you do in the areas where you are skilled.

4. Over the next year, if you consistently invest as much effort into the areas where your skills are lacking as you would for the areas where you are skilled, how many sales would this Dare earn you? Circle one:

     .25 sales   .5 sales   .75 sales   1 sale

     1.25 sales   1.5 sales   1.75 sales   2 sales

effort

Rate your effort level towards improving yourself today with this Dare:

1   2   3   4   5   6   7   8   9   10

1: Did not read or do the Dare. 2: Read the Dare, but did not do it. 5: Did the Dare with half of my customers today. 10: Did the Dare with all customers today, and rehearsed the questions between customer encounters.

Dare 40

Stump Me Twice, Shame on Me

read

How would your interactions with customers change if you knew that you'd never hear an objection? In that lovely world, would you show that home site that backs up to the railroad tracks more often? Would you make your follow-up calls more frequently and fearlessly? Would you feel more confident? Let's face it, you're not going to be a very effective salesperson if you let fear of objections keep you from, well, from *selling*.

This lesson is twofold. First, work as if you're not afraid of objections. Second, since you know that you will have objections, take ownership of your career by being as prepared as possible to address them. You should always have answers ready for the objections you can anticipate. But what about those stumpers that are bound to come your way? Those are your biggest opportunities to turn a No into a Yes. When someone hands you a stumper, it's okay not to have an answer right then. Yes, I said it's okay... the *first time* (stump me once, shame on you). But it's not okay the second time (stump me twice, shame on me). So *find* answers. Look on the Internet, ask your sales manager, do whatever it takes—just make sure you do *something* so that the next time a customer has the same objection, it doesn't stump you.

In short: work as if you're not afraid of objections; but when you get one, don't let it stump you twice.

"Stumpers" are my biggest opportunity to turn a No into a Yes.

Work as if I'm not afraid of objections.

t h i n k

When was the last time your fear of objections limited your sales presentation? What would you have done differently if you hadn't had that fear?

_____

_____

_____

_____

D A R E

I dare you today to write a list of all the objections that have stumped you in the past. Pick the three most frequent ones, and find a solution to each by the end of today. When you find the solution, say it aloud. This will increase your confidence, as well as the probability that you'll remember and use that solution the next time the same objection comes up.

r e f l e c t

1. What do you think about a salesperson when you present them with an objection they cannot answer?

_____

_____

_____

_____

_____

_____

_____

2. Why do you believe you have procrastinated in the past when trying to uncover a solution to an objection that stumped you?

_____

_____

_____

_____

_____

_____

3. With your prospects today, were you able to use your solutions to your most frequent objections? What happened?

_____

_____

_____

_____

_____

_____

_____

4. What did you learn about yourself from this Dare?

_____

_____

_____

_____

_____

_____

_____

5. If you consistently execute this Dare with every objection you encounter over the next year, how many sales would this Dare earn you? Circle one:

    .25 sales   .5 sales   .75 sales   1 sale

    1.25 sales   1.5 sales   1.75 sales   2 sales

effort

Rate your effort level towards improving yourself today with this Dare:

1   2   3   4   5   6   7   8   9   10

1: Did not read or do the Dare. 2: Read the Dare, but did not do it. 5: Did the Dare with half of my customers today. 10: Did the Dare with all customers today, and rehearsed the questions between customer encounters.

Week 6 Summary

Before you complete your journey, you need to take a moment to complete your Week 6 Summary. **You must do this in order to complete the "What's it Worth" equation on page 233.**

Average Effort Score for Week 6:

Review your Effort Scores from Dares 36-40, and calculate your Average Effort Score for the week. Write it in the space below.

_____

What's it worth?

What was this week worth to you? Flip back through Week 6, and tally the number of sales that you said Dares 36-40 would earn you. Write it below.

_____

You did it!
You completed all 40 Dares!

Now turn the page to calculate the potential value of this program.

How Much Effort Did You Give?

Very quickly, go look up your Effort averages for Weeks 1-6, and write them in the spaces below.

_____ Week 1

_____ Week 2

_____ Week 3

_____ Week 4

_____ Week 5

_____ Week 6

Now, add up your scores and divide the total by 6 to calculate your average Effort Score for *40 Day Sales Dare.* Write your Effort Score below.

_____

Now you know how much you need to step up your effort in order to maximize the impact of *40 Day Sales Dare,* and achieve your full potential. If your average score is anything less than 10, then I strongly advise that you repeat the program for your benefit. Trust me on this. I want you to see how much you stand to gain if you were to keep applying the Dares until you gave them 100% of your effort, so continue to the next page for some very important calculations.

What's It Worth?

What is this book worth to you? Flip back through your Summary Pages for Weeks 1-6, and calculate the total number of sales that you could earn if you executed all forty Dares with 100% effort. Write your total below.

If I follow everything in this book, and give 100% effort, I have the potential to earn _____ sales this year.

Now, calculate how much money you could earn if you executed everything that you learned from *40 Day Sales Dare for New Home Sales***:**

_____	* $_____	= $_____
# of sales you have the potential to earn by executing all forty Dares	your average commission per house	What you could earn.

To fully realize the meaning of that potential, I want you to complete the sentence below and answer the question that follows:

If I follow everything in this book, and give 100% effort, I have the potential to earn $_____.

1. What would this money mean to you and your family?

_____

_____

_____

_____

_____

_____

_____

_____

If you want to reach this income goal, I believe you can do it if you commit to mastering the Dares in this book, and giving 100% effort. If you'd like, you can simply go through the book again, and repeat the Dares that you know you need to improve upon.

Or, you can make a fresh start and follow a new path through *40 Day Sales Dare*. On the next two pages, there is a Topic Outline that divides the Dares into four categories. By following this outline, you can concentrate on one major theme at a time. Also, this time around, you can set your own schedule. You still need to do the Day-On Dares when you're in the office but, because of the way this outline is structured, you don't have to wait for your days off to work on the Day-Off Dares. Just work them into your schedule as you see fit. After you've completed a Dare and feel that you've given it your 100% best effort, check it off the list.

What is this book worth to you? I want to know!

Send me an e-mail and tell me how much money you have the potential to earn as a result of *40 Day Sales Dare*. Also, feel free to share what these earnings would mean to you and your family, and what you plan to do in order to make this a reality. And, when you reach your goal, I want to hear about it!

Email your stories to: Jason@ShoreForrest.com

Note to self:
Have Jason personally hold me accountable through
"40 Day Sales Dare University" at www.40DaySalesDare.com.

Topic Outline

Mental Motivation

Understanding the Customer's Mission to Improve Their Life

* Because of the structure of this outline, you may execute the Day-Off Dares when you are in the office, i.e. you don't have to wait for your days off to do them.

Solving the Customer's Mission to Improve Their Life

Holding the Customer Accountable to Achieving Their Mission

About the Author

Jason Forrest is an accomplished sales trainer, consultant and author whose passion is transforming homebuilders into high-performance sales teams, and their sales representatives into high-performance sales athletes. He believes that true sales training changes not only companies, but also people's lives as they learn how to reach their full potential. Jason's vision for Shore Forrest is to partner with homebuilding organizations who are tired of market circumstances affecting their short- and long-term sales goals. Jason currently spends the majority of his week tele-coaching sales managers, division presidents and company owners on how to overcome the tough market challenges they face.

The former National Director of Sales Development for MDC Holdings/ Richmond American Homes, Jason has extensive experience in new home sales and sales management. He holds an MBA in marketing, a degree in psychology, and a 'Certified New Home Sales Professional' designation from the NAHB—a perfect combination for dealing with the tough housing market he knows so well.

Jason is President of Shore Forrest Sales Strategies, providing the industry's best coaching and training services for homebuilding companies around North America. He is the author of *Creating Urgency in a Non-Urgent Housing Market* and *40 Day Sales Dare for New Home Sales* and, together with Jeff Shore, is the co-creator of Leadership Selling® and Leadership Selling® for Coaches, a 33-week blended-learning training curriculum for new home sales.

Jason resides in Fort Worth, Texas, with his wife, Shelly, his children, Saunders and Mary Jane, and a Goldendoodle named Happy.

Linked in. www.linkedin.com/in/JasonForrest

 twitter.com/jforrestspeaker | youtube: www.youtube.com/jasonforrest

www.JasonForrestSpeaker.com | Jason@ShoreForrest.com

40 day sales
DARE
UNIVERSITY

for New Home Sales

Take the impact of *40 Day Sales Dare* to a higher level through this six-week, live, interactive video coaching program with Jason Forrest.

Learn more at

www.40DaySalesDare.com

LEADERSHIP SELLING®

Leadership Selling® is not just a seminar—it's a three-level system, taking salespeople to a higher level of skill than is possible with a typical one-level program. Each level consists of 11 weekly lessons, to include:

Education
through weekly, interactive 30-minute online instruction.

Experiential Learning
through 'Real Play' and weekly assignments in the *Leadership Selling®* Handbook.

Role Plays
to rehearse the weekly assignments.

One-on-One Coaching
from Sales Managers.

Watch Informational Videos at
www.LeadershipSelling.com

Creating Urgency in a Non-Urgent Housing Market
Jason Forrest

Tough Market New Home Sales
Jeff Shore

Deal With It!
Jeff Shore

Outstanding Sales Meetings
Jeff Shore

Training Opportunities

Contact us at 40DaySalesDare.com, or email us at info@ShoreForrest.com to learn how to:

- Enroll in *40 Day Sales Dare University*.

- Invite Jason Forrest to give a keynote on *40 Day Sales Dare for New Home Sales*.

- Inquire about Shore Forrest's training and consulting services, including Leadership Selling®.

* * *

Ordering Information

To order additional copies of *40 Day Sales Dare for New Home Sales*, please visit www.40DaySalesDare.com. A bulk discount is applied to orders of 10 or more. To order in bulk, please contact info@ShoreForrest.com.

* * *

Tell Us Your Story

Were you impacted by this book? After applying its principles, have you had any experiences that you would like to share?

We at Shore Forrest are passionate about helping sales professionals transform the way they sell and the way they live. If you have a success story, we'd love to hear it!

Send your success stories to:
info@ShoreForrest.com